Praise for *Through Thorns I Thrive*

"A daring exposé of Carla's most important journey—the voyage from her ego, separation, and aloneness to the one she really is. It is a wonderful example of one's actual life being the pathway home."

Stephen Garrett
Author, *When Death Speaks*

"Carla courageously exposes her life's lessons and gifts them to all readers displaying that there is hope when one chooses to uncover their emotional blocks, clear them and incorporate proven methodologies and techniques to achieve a state of happiness and well being that all humans desire. Her journey could be your journey and as such a healing path awaits the reader."

Kieron Sweeney
Mindset Coach and Transformational Trainer

"This book is food for your soul. I laughed, I cried, and I felt deeply touched, moved, and inspired. As you read through the pages you will be swept away on a heartfelt journey from challenges to blessings in disguise."

Darren Jacklin
Professional Speaker, Corporate Trainer, Angel Investor
www.DarrenJacklin.com

"*We are born for a very important reason. No one is exempt from that. Carla's personal journey will give so many people permission to find their courage to discover just how amazing and important they are to all of Humanity! Share this book with someone who can benefit from the intimate inspiration that Carla generously gives.*"

Deborah M Borges, LSC, RHN
Personal Responsibility Expert

"*Carla's book is an inspiring lesson on how you can turn your life around with hard work. This book reminded me about all the strategies she has taught me through her life courses that have helped me to be positive and grateful. It is truly from her soul; thank you for sharing your passion with the world. My hope is that she can reach more people like myself, to change their lives and the ones around them. Thank you, Thank you, Thank you!*"

Your biggest fan,
Donna Hagglund, wife and mother

"Through Thorns I Thrive *is a journey taken through the heart of a woman who found the courage to overcome many of the challenges we as mothers, sisters, and wives are forced to confront at one time or another in our lives. Carla's story is heartrending and real, transforming and inspiring.*"

Sandy Bucholtz
Author, *Letters From Heaven Love Mom xo*
www.sandybucholtz.com

"A spiritual, heartfelt journey from chaos to coherence. Carla has written a heartfelt narrative of a life worth the struggle when it leads to happiness and love."

Christopher Cribb
Certified LifeSuccess Consultant~Recruiter
Certified Passion Test Facilitator
www.christophercribb.lifesuccessconsultants.com

"Through Thorns I Thrive is a book that, once you start, you can't put down! It's inspiring and touches the reader in a personal way. As we read each well-written chapter we were pulled deeper into the candid story of Carla's life. By opening her heart and soul she helps us all see that we are human and we can choose to believe in ourselves and our capacity to conquer life struggles. Carla lovingly provides hope, understanding, and guidance to the hurting or struggling soul."

Rick and Leisa Olson
Parent/Family Coaches, Authors, Creators of the F.U.S.E. Family
Programs, and Certified LifeSuccess Consultants

Kelly,

I THROUGH THORNS
I THRIVE

*A Spiritual Journey through the Depths of
Hell to Finding Heaven Here on Earth*

*Thanks so much, you
continue to inspire me.
Keep on & Thrive On!*

CARLA LINDGREN COATES

BALBOA
PRESS
A DIVISION OF HAY HOUSE

*Love
Carla*

Balboa Press books may be ordered through booksellers or by contacting:

Balboa Press
A Division of Hay House
1663 Liberty Drive
Bloomington, IN 47403
www.balboapress.com
1-(877) 407-4847

Printed in the United States of America.

ISBN: 978-1-4525-7452-3 (sc)
ISBN: 978-1-4525-7453-0 (e)

Balboa Press rev. date: 6/4/2013

This book is written for anyone who suffers from depression or loss. May you find the light. The love of God will take you there and heal your heart.

The Rose

Some say love, it is a river that drowns a tender reed
Some say love, it is a razor that leaves your soul to bleed
Some say love, it is a hunger, an endless aching need
I say love it is a flower, and you it's only seed

It's the heart afraid of breaking that never learns to dance
And the dream afraid of waking that never takes a chance
It's the one who won't be taken, that can not seem to give
And the soul afraid of dying, that never learns to live

When the night has been to lonely and
the road has been to long
And you think that love is only for the lucky and the strong
Just remember in the winter far beneath the bitter snow
Lies a seed that with the suns love, in
the spring becomes the rose.

Amanda McBroom

CONTENTS

FOREWORD

Have you ever felt unhappy or that your life wasn't what you thought it would be? Are you always searching for more happiness and not finding it? Whether you know it yet or not, it is your birthright as a human being to live a purposeful and passionate life.

The book you hold in your hand is a simple, yet profound example of how it is possible to change your life no matter what your circumstances.

It all begins with the thoughts you think about yourself. Most people think there is a world out there separate from themselves. They fall into the trap that creates fear, suffering, and unhappiness. Yet you have a choice.

What you believe, you will create. What would you rather believe? That life will always be difficult and disappointing or that the universe is full of abundance and adventure? Would you rather live a mediocre and automatic life, or a magnificent and authentic one? Would you rather believe the world is a dangerous place or that everything and everyone in it is here to support you on your journey?

You have the ability to choose what you think and what you believe. If you are not happy with the way things are, you have the ability to change, just the way Carla did.

When you begin to be grateful for the things you have, and appreciate that every moment on this earth is a gift, you will find more joy. What you put your attention on grows stronger in your life.

Finding your passions and following your heart will lead you effortlessly on to fulfill your unique and special purpose for being alive. When you are living on purpose, you are aligned with your destiny. You have special gifts given to you so you may share them with the world. When you share your gifts with others, both your life and theirs will be richer.

Through Thorns I Thrive is a perfect example that life is a magnificent journey. We all have difficulties in our life, but we can choose how we react and learn the lessons they are meant to teach us. It is our natural state to shine and thrive, and grow stronger through our trials. Everything you experience is what makes you who you are. Embrace your true nature. It is never too late to discover who you are or why you are here. Once you do you will never look back.

Chris Attwood, co-author of the *New York Times* bestseller *The Passion Test: The Effortless Path to Discovering Your Life Purpose*

PREFACE

When we are no longer able to change a situation,
we are challenged to change ourselves.

~Viktor Frankl

When I was a young girl, I watched the movie *The Rose*, based on the life of Janis Joplin and starring Bette Midler. Bette plays Mary Rose Foster, a young woman whose music career is beginning to take off. Throughout the movie we witness her wonderful, exciting life as she goes on to fame, fortune, and a life some only dream about.

Then, as sometimes happens, the fame becomes too much for her, and she starts to spiral out of control. She turns to drugs and alcohol, which destroys her career, relationships, and, in the end, her life.

I loved the movie, especially the theme song, "The Rose." I grew up in a musical family, so music has always been a part of my life—a passion even. Music moves me and touches my soul, and singing helps me express my feelings. So shortly after seeing the movie I bought the music and lyrics for "The Rose." I came home, sat down at the piano, and learned to play it.

One day my dad heard me singing it and said, "That is a beautiful song, Carla." From then on, any time I sat at the piano, he would ask me to sing it. My mom and sisters would harmonize with me. It became my trademark, and even now, years later, anytime we have a family get-together, when the guitars come out, I am requested to sing "The Rose."

Funny thing is, for all those years I sang the song, I never really resonated with the true meaning of the words. Now, I am blown away by how it has represented my life.

I struggled for years with low self-esteem, depression, and obesity. I never felt good enough, and I thought I didn't matter—I thought there was something wrong with me. Shortly after my thirtieth birthday, I remember getting up one morning and sitting on the edge of my bed, feeling as if the life had drained out of me. I had had short bouts of depression prior to this, but this precipitated what became fifteen long, agonizing years of feeling totally empty. My life had no meaning; I felt as if I was just going through the motions.

I didn't want to live, but I was afraid to die. I always seemed to be searching and yearning for something, but I didn't know what. Something was missing. I felt as if there were a hole or void in my heart, and I didn't know what it was.

I tried filling the void with food, but it never took away the emptiness I felt inside. I was always looking for answers, always doubting, and had very little faith. As a child I had gone to church every Sunday, but I grew up fearing God, believing I was a sinner and that I'd be punished for my sins. As an adult I really struggled with religion. I was angry with God for everything he had put me through. *No God would do that; there is no such thing as God!* I thought.

When my life was as bad as it could be, while I was completely lost in the abyss, my dad died. Although I almost went over the edge, that event created "the shift" I needed to move from darkness and despair to joy and happiness again.

I have heard it said from the darkest moments come the greatest gifts, and that often it is our deepest pain that empowers us to grow into our highest self.

My life is a true testimony to that. This is my story of how I went from lost and broken, struggling through obstacles, wandering aimlessly through a life with no meaning, to one of joy, happiness, and fulfillment, finding not only God but myself. It is my wish that if you have ever felt the same, my story will help you through *your* thorns so that you too may thrive.

Just remember in the winter far beneath the bitter snow,
Lies a seed that with the sun's love, in
the spring becomes the rose.

From "The Rose," music and lyrics
by Amanda McBroom

Acknowledgements

There are so many people I want to acknowledge that were involved in my journey.

First of all, I would like to thank my family. You are the most important people in my life. We have been through many struggles and losses together and we have always had unconditional love for one other. The bond we have is precious and rare, and I am so grateful for that. This is our book, not mine.

To my parents, Vern and Irene Lindgren, thank you for teaching me and our entire family the most important thing—that which conquers all—LOVE. I miss you, Dad, and love you, Mom. You are truly my inspiration.

To my siblings, Elaine, Diane, Koreen, Calvin, Phyllis, Kim and Garth. You have always been and will always be my best friends, confidants, and biggest fans. I love you with all my heart.

Also, to your spouses, Warn, Wendy, Bob, Clarence, and Janice, I love you all as brothers and sisters.

To my beautiful nieces, Jodie, Charlene, Tanice, Lacey, Ashley, Kari, and Melissa. I am so proud of the strong, confident women you have become.

To my nephews, Trevor, Darcie, Jeff, Geordie, Devlon, Dale, Terry, Myron, and Chad. You are smart, handsome, loving men, and I am very proud to be your aunt.

To those we have lost, Dad, Herman, BJ, and Kayden. You will be in our hearts forever; we miss you and know you are watching over us.

To Wes, thank you for all the love and support you gave me. You will always be my very dear friend.

To Chris, even though I did not give birth to you, you will always be my son. I love you very much and am more proud of you than you will ever know.

To my friends of more than thirty years, Tracy, Bonnie and Lori, we don't see each other often, but when we do it's as if we were together yesterday. I will value our friendship always.

Phyllis, thank you for being my business partner and taking the journey of self-discovery along with me. Your wisdom and loving support never falter.

To Melissa, Phyllis, Kim, Koreen, and my friend Martin Presse, thank you all for reviewing my manuscript and providing me your feedback. I appreciate the time, effort and insight you gave me. Special thanks goes to my editor, Jennifer Read Hawthorne. Your skill and talent knowing exactly what I wanted to say and making my words flow was incredible.

Also thanks to Charmaine Hammond and Teresa de Grosbois for your knowledge and teachings, which helped me reach my goals with this book.

To all of my other mentors and teachers along the way: Bob Proctor and my LifeSuccess Family; Chris Attwood and Janet Attwood and The Passion Test family; Jay Fisset and Rae-Ann Wood-Schatz and the Creators Code family; Adam Markel and Kieron Sweeney and my Peak Potentials family; Stephen Garratt; Les Brown; and Mark Victor Hansen. I am very grateful to have been in the presence of such visionaries and like-minded loving people. With you in my life, I have grown exponentially.

To mentors I have had but have not had the opportunity to meet yet, Dr. Wayne Dyer and Rhonda Byrne, you are both my idols and I have set the intention to meet you someday.

To Mark, thank you for supporting me, listening to me, and loving me through this process. You have proven to me that true love can happen more than once in a lifetime.

And last but most important, thank you, God, for coming into my heart, healing me, and giving me this miraculous gift called life.

PART I

THE DEPTHS OF HELL

We do not heal the past by dwelling there,
we heal the past by living fully in the present.

~Marianne Williamson

CHAPTER 1

GOING TO THE DOGS

Let me start by introducing you to my family and my childhood, as they play an important role not only in my life, but also the things I'm going to share with you in this book. Depression for me started at a young age, in a highly disciplined family structure that exposed my siblings and me to arduous labour as we endeavored to fulfill my father's dreams.

I was born in Edmonton, Alberta, where I lived for the first six years of my life.

I am the second youngest of eight children. Although we were not poor, my parents seemed to struggle to make ends meet and to put food on the table. In his younger years, my dad owned his own plumbing business. Later on, he worked at union jobs as a pipe fitter. I was afraid of him as a child. He was a strict disciplinarian and when he spoke, we knew he meant business. He seemed to be harder on the older kids, but as the years went by, he softened. Even with his rough exterior, he was never afraid to tell us he loved us, and he did it often.

My mom, on the other hand, was soft-spoken, gentle, and kind. People called her Sweet Irene. My dad worshiped her and expected the same from us kids. She was the strong, silent type, the rock of our family. While Dad worked, she stayed home to run the house and raise us. Raising eight kids can't be easy, but she did it with love and patience. She worked as we grew older, but she was always there when we were young children.

Seven Siblings

I have five sisters and two brothers. I was only six years old when my oldest sister, Elaine, left home and married her husband Herman (I was the flower girl for their wedding). I always remember Elaine looking after us kids. To this day, she still calls me "baby sister." Elaine and Herman had two boys, Trevor and Darcie.

Diane was the next oldest. She was the quiet one. She did get married, but it was a very abusive relationship and ended after only a few short years. She had two children as well, Jodie and Jeff.

Then came my sister Koreen. To me she always seemed to be the calm and level-headed one. Her first marriage to George was a very unhappy one. She had three children with him, Geordie, Charlene, and BJ. When BJ was only a couple of years old, Koreen divorced George and met and married the love of her life, Warn, who also had a son, Devlon.

My brother Calvin was my big brother, my protector. I remember when I was little and was upset about something, he would sit me on his knee and comfort me. He'd say, "Why are you crying?" and tell me everything would be okay. He married Wendy and had three children, Dale, Terry, and Tanice.

Phyllis was next in line. She was named so perfectly I think. I call her Phyllis the Philosopher, because, in my eyes, she has always been so wise, always knowing the right thing to do and say. She stepped in and took the role of "Mother" to the rest of us whenever mom wasn't around. She married Bob and had two children, Myron and Lacey.

Kim is the sister closest in age to me, the bubbly one. She is a people person and loves being with her family and friends. She married Clarence and had two girls, Ashley and Kari.

Next comes me. I won't go into detail here, as this book will tell my story.

Last but not least is Garth, my little brother. As kids, I always thought he was so spoiled and such a little bugger. He was the biggest tease. He would sit on me and make me so mad I would cry. We fought like cats and dogs when we were little kids. But as we grew up and became teenagers, we hung out and became best friends. He was the one to always make us laugh, with his sharp wit and sense of humor. Garth married Janice and had two children, Melissa and Chad.

We have always been a very close and loving family, and all of my brothers and sisters are like friends to me. They're my biggest supporters, and I can confide in any one of them if I need to. Many people have commented throughout the years on how close we are and have said they wished they had what we do. Even our extended family—aunts, uncles, and cousins—are close. We are very blessed, and for that I am grateful.

Depression Comes Early

Because there were so many of us in one household, you can imagine the chaos at meal time and getting ready for school or other outings. Being the disciplinarian my dad was, we were always told to "be quiet and behave." I remember hearing the phrase more than once that "children should be seen and not heard." I always felt that I wasn't allowed to speak and say what I needed to say. I felt I had to keep my thoughts and feelings inside, to myself.

I remember the first time I felt depressed. It was in the first grade. I would not have considered it depression back then, but I remember a period when I felt very sad. I didn't want to attend school, and I told my mom I wasn't feeling well so I wouldn't have to go.

There was one period when I missed about two weeks of school. My mom finally forced me to go back. But again, I didn't want to be there. After a couple of hours I told my teacher I was sick and had to go home. I remember her looking at me with a very stern look on her face, as if I were a bad girl, and asking, "What's wrong with you?" For many years after, those words echoed in my head; I was always thinking there was something "wrong" with me.

City Kids to Country Bumpkins

In the summer after first grade, my mom, dad, and seven of us kids left Edmonton and moved to Whitecourt to pursue my dad's dream of owning a farm. My oldest sister, Elaine, had just gotten married. She would later move to Whitecourt with Herman and their boys.

We had no idea what we were getting into. We were city kids moving to a small farm three miles outside a very small town. But we had no choice but to all pile into an old panel van and make the journey to our new home.

I remember our shock as we pulled into town. It was so small! There was nothing here—no streetlights, no bus stops, and no shopping malls. When we turned up the road towards our new "homestead," we were even more surprised. It was more like a path in the bush instead of a road: two tire tracks with grass growing in between them. Trees hung over the road like umbrellas shading the path to our new home.

The only other inhabitants on this country road were our neighbours, the Cartwrights, a family of five boys.

When we got to our farm, there, in the middle of an overgrown meadow, we saw a poured basement of four concrete walls and an old broken down Edmonton Transit bus. That was it! There was no house or even a garden shed. We were all puzzled; the culture shock was overwhelming. "Where are we going to live?" my sister Kim asked my dad. He said, "Right there," pointing to the old bus.

What? Our jaws dropped and our eyes grew big with disbelief. Here we were, seven kids and my parents, about to embark on a "camping" trip, which would last several months. We were city kids one day and country bumpkins the next.

During the summer, while camping in the bus, we built a roof over the basement, hooked up a wood stove, built an outhouse, and cleared some land. When winter came, we moved into the basement. On one side of the basement were the kitchen and living quarters. The other side served as the bedroom, where five beds where we all slept were lined up in a row. During the summer we slept under plastic draped over our beds to keep us dry, because the rain would leak through the temporary roof. Our only source of heat was the wood stove; we had no running water, and TV and phone were luxuries we would do without for many years.

All the other kids I went to school with had TVs and telephones and nice houses to live in. It was 1967, after all, not the 1930s! But we lived like settlers from the "olden" days, the way Mom and Dad had lived when they grew up. Our long list of chores consisted of hauling water, gathering and chopping wood, and picking roots in the field Dad had cleared so that he could grow hay for the collection of farm animals he brought home.

That is how we lived for several years. Our family worked very hard, especially my brother Calvin. He was the oldest boy, and my dad expected a lot from him—maybe too much from a boy of sixteen.

Calvin hated laundry and bath days, because it meant that much more water to haul. To conserve water we would all bathe, one at a time, in an old steel washtub. This was done on Sunday nights so we would all be clean to go to school the next day. Luckily, being second youngest, the water was still fairly clean when it was my turn to bathe, as Garth was the only one to use it before me. We were first because we had to go to bed earlier.

My older siblings, however, didn't have it so good, because my mom would just keep adding warm water for each kid to bathe in. Rather disgusting to think about it now! I really pitied the last one in.

It took mom and dad (and us kids) fourteen years to completely finish building the house. To my mom and older siblings, it may have felt like a prison sentence; to me it was an adventure. I was only seven years old, and my younger brother Garth and I didn't have to work as hard as our older siblings did.

We did, however, work harder than most kids our age—but we had a lot of fun doing it. To take the focus off the grueling labor, we would make games out of our chores. One day while we were loading some hay, Garth and I were arguing. He was really annoying me, as he loved to do, and I lightly poked him with the pitchfork I had in my hand so he would stop his teasing.

His version of the story is very different from mine, however. He says I threw the pitch fork at him, which made the sound "donnnnggggg," as it stuck in his back and vibrated back and forth. We still laugh about it today whenever he tells the story.

Although I learned a lot during those years, my every day was what kids my age only heard about from grandparents or learned in history class at school. But it was normal for me. I was young enough to adapt to this lifestyle. But I was embarrassed to bring friends home, because I didn't want any one to know how we lived.

My Ninth Birthday

On my ninth birthday, however, I decided I wanted to have a birthday party. I invited six or seven kids from school and around the neighborhood. I don't remember much about the party, except for what happened that day would impact my life for many years to come.

My dad raised huskies. In the summer we would go to dog shows, where he would proudly show off his beautiful dogs. In the winter he would travel around the province, racing his huskies via dog sled. Of course, riding on the dog sled was always a highlight for us kids. I learned at a very early age the meaning of the word *mush*.

As a small child, I remember these big dogs being somewhat aggressive. In fact, they would sometimes bowl me over with their energy. But overall they were friendly.

On this particular day in March, my ninth birthday, we had finished the cake, presents, and all the formalities. We were outside playing and one of the kids said, "Let's go pet the dogs!" We trotted down to where my dad kept the dogs tied up on tethers, several hundred feet away from the house.

The dogs got very excited and barked and yelped and tried to jump up on us. Some of the kids were afraid of them. One little girl, however, was not afraid at all. She was very small in stature, and she walked right up to one of the huge huskies. She petted him with a big smile on her face.

All of a sudden the dog grabbed her by the arm with his mouth, pulling her in closer. He flopped her around like a rag

9

doll, viciously mauling her. I can still hear her screaming and crying. I was terrified!

I couldn't do anything to help her by myself, so I ran up to the house screaming: "Help, Seanna is being attacked by Sheba!" Luckily, my older sister Phyllis was outside; she heard the screams and ran to Seanna, grabbing the dog's chain and pulling at it until she had the dog by the head. Each time she'd try to get the dog to release Seanna, she'd tell me to pull her away. Each time I did, Seanna's skin would tear where the dog's teeth pierced her.

After what seemed an eternity, Phyllis tackled the dog to the ground and, by placing her knee on the side of the dog's jaw, forced it to let go. I then pulled Seanna out of the dog's reach to safety.

There on the ground was this little girl, covered in blood, with gashes all over her frail little body; one or two millimeters more, the dog would have punctured her jugular vein. Phyllis picked Seanna up and ran with her to the house. As luck would have it, the two vehicles my Dad owned were both out of commission; one had a flat tire, and the other wouldn't start. We couldn't get her to the hospital!

So my older brother Calvin jumped on our horse and, in full gallop, raced the three miles to town. As he got to town he flagged down the first vehicle, which miraculously was the town doctor. He put the reins around the horse's neck, slapped her hindquarters, and pointed her towards home. Then he jumped into the doctor's car and brought him back to our house.

Seanna ended up having over one hundred stitches to mend all her wounds. I remember her mom, Lynne, coming to our house later that evening and asking me what had happened. I was hysterical, sobbing uncontrollably and barely able to get the words out. I remember saying through my sobs, "I uh . . . uh . . . uh . . . was uh . . . uh . . . uh . . . terrified." Seanna's mother smiled at me and assured me it was not my fault. But my dad sold the dogs soon after.

Several weeks later Phyllis got a call from the province telling her she had won an award for bravery. A neighbor and close friend from the community had submitted her name for the Grant MacEwan Junior Citizenship award. She went to Edmonton and was presented the award by Grant MacEwan, the Lieutenant Governor of the province.

There was a write-up in the local paper of how this young, brave fourteen-year-old girl had rescued a little girl from a vicious dog attack. My sister was a celebrity in our little town. She received praise from everyone, including my parents, who of course were very proud of her.

I was very proud of her, too; I mean who wouldn't be. I looked up to my big sister. But with all the attention and glory and accolades she received over the rescue incident, not once was my brother's or my involvement in the rescue mentioned. Nothing in the papers revealed that fact. And no one, not even our parents, ever acknowledged the part we had played in the rescue.

I felt I was a nobody. I didn't matter. I carried so much guilt for taking the kids to the dogs in the first place, it felt like a poison inside me. If I hadn't done that, Seanna wouldn't have been hurt. I had made a very bad mistake.

Years later, in my twenties, I confronted my parents and sister and told them how belittled that experience made me feel. They were sympathetic and apologized, not having realized the impact that event had had on me. All I had wanted was to be validated and acknowledged. All I had wanted was to be given some credit for helping to save that little girl.

Then, just a few short years ago, events (which you'll read about) happened that enabled me to let it go. I realized that the resentment I was holding onto was serving no purpose; all it was doing was eating at me like a cancer—and the only person it was hurting was me. I could not change what had happened on that day so many years ago, but I could change my feelings towards it.

I learned to confront issues head on, rather than letting them boil inside me. I learned not to allow the fear to stop me from facing my issues and dealing with them. I also learned that many times we suffer in silence, and other people don't even know that what they did or said caused us pain. It's often unintentional on their part, but if they know how we're feeling, they can give us the compassion to help us heal.

After sharing the feelings that I had kept inside for so many years with my mom and sister, I made the conscious decision to let it go. I understand now that in choosing to do this, it released me from the suffering and helped me move on.

CHAPTER 2

LIFE'S NOT SO BAD

Achieve your dreams a day at a time.
Set goals for each day.

~Og Mandino

Several years passed, and my life was typical of a teenager growing up in small town Alberta. After high school I moved back and forth from Edmonton to Whitecourt several times, trying to find my place in life. I had two or three not-so-serious relationships during that time, and I worked several jobs, mostly administrative.

About ten years later, in 1987, I was feeling that my life wasn't going anywhere. Again I felt depressed; my career wasn't giving me the satisfaction I was looking for. I wanted a job that would pay enough so I could support myself and never need to rely on anyone else.

So I decided to go back to school. I enrolled in Health Record Administration at the Northern Alberta Institute of Technology, where I studied for two years.

After graduating from college, my life began merrily rolling along. It seemed as if whatever I put my mind to, I did. I set goals for my career and achieved them. My first job out of college was in Athabasca, a small town north of Edmonton. My preceptor had recommended me for the position—and I got the job: Director of the Health Records department in the hospital there. Really? How does someone like me get a job as director with no experience? I was fresh out of college!

I worked there for a year, but honestly, I had no clue what I was doing. I had no idea how to manage a department. I was just really good at faking it—even though I felt unsure of my decisions and myself.

Two weeks after moving to Athabasca, I went to visit my girlfriend Tracy, who lived in Camrose at the time. It was there that I met Wes. He was a strong, husky guy with curly, red hair. About a week or so later we went out on our first date; he told me he had been married before and had a son, Christopher. Just the way Wes talked about his son made me fall in love with him. His son meant everything to him; he was his whole world.

The first time I met Christopher, I fell in love with him too. He was three years old, dressed in blue jeans, shirt, cowboy boots, and a cowboy hat. He walked right up to me, shook my hand, and said, "My name is Chwistopho"—not being able to fully enunciate his r's yet.

Wes and Christopher lived in Edmonton, about an hour and a half away. Every weekend I would drive to Edmonton to see them. After a year, our relationship started to get serious—but I was getting tired of the drive. I was also lonely living in Athabasca, as I hadn't made many friends there. So I quit my job and moved back to Edmonton.

It took me a while to find something in my field; in fact, I was without work for a couple of months. This meant trouble: I became bored and started eating. I'd always been able to manage weight and had never had a weight problem prior to this. But after moving to Edmonton I started to pack the pounds on.

After some time I found a temporary position at a junior level (where most people would have started). After being director of a department, I was now starting over. I'm sure my childhood experiences had something to do with how this made me feel: very inadequate.

It was just a temporary setback, though. Looking back on my life, I realize that although I felt inadequate at times and had a few stumbling blocks, I always had a clear vision of where I wanted to be in my career and was always able to reach my goals. I had honors in both school and college, received a scholarship in college, and got that department director position right after graduating. Later I became a regional analyst, and now I have a provincial position.

I didn't know it back then, but it proves that when you're clear about what you want, and set goals and intentions, things fall into place. Unknowingly, I was able to do this with my career. It was one thing that came easily for me.

I just couldn't seem to apply it to the rest of my life.

CHAPTER 3

BABIES, PRECIOUS BABIES

Life is not fair—get used to it.

~Bill Gates

Wes and I dated four years and then were married. We were so in love! I absolutely adored him and he me. Soon after the wedding, as my biological clock ticked very loudly in my head, we decided to have children. I was in my thirties, after all.

It had always been my dream as a little girl, as it is for many, to find the love of my life, get married, and have children. I was very excited. I was also afraid. Wes already had Chris, so he didn't share the same excitement I did, but he was definitely ready to have another child.

I went off birth control and we started our pursuit of making a baby. Here I was a mature woman, with a wonderful husband, both with good, stable jobs, and soon I would also be a mother. I had never been happier in my life. Life was good!

A couple of weeks went by and I got my period. We knew we weren't pregnant yet. "Oh well, we'll try again next month" was my attitude, fully expecting it would take a month or two. Another month went by. Again, I was disappointed but remained positive. Several more months went by, and I still wasn't pregnant.

With each passing month I became more depressed. Each month I seemed to mourn the loss of the baby that never came. It was excruciatingly painful. The more depressed I became, the more I ate; the more I ate, the more weight I gained.

Then there were the times when my mom and dad came over to visit. We would be chatting away and, one day, as many parents do, Dad asked, "So when are you going to give me a grandchild?" My heart sank in my chest. I quietly answered "Actually, we've been trying for a while, but nothing's happened yet." He never asked again.

Others also asked, "When are you going to have kids?" Each time I would get more aggravated and irritated; it was really starting to piss me off!

A year went by. Wes and I decided we should get tested. We talked about it for days, especially about the semen sample he'd have to give. Frankly, Wes was scared to get the test done. He was quite shy when it came to sex, even around me.

The day came for our appointment. We walked into the doctor's office, went up to the receptionist, who, with a smiling face, asked, "Hello, what are you here for today?" I thought Wes was going to have a heart attack. His face went beet red, he was so embarrassed. I spoke up because I knew he wouldn't be able to, and said, "We're here for fertility testing."

We waited a while, which seems to be the norm when you go to the doctor. We read magazines, we talked about our day, and we shuffled in our seats. When we were finally called into the doctor's office, he talked with us for a few moments and explained how the testing would be done. He then handed Wes a plastic cup with a lid and told him to go home, do whatever he needed to do to give the sample—then drive it to a nearby lab. It had to be there within half an hour, or they wouldn't be able to test the sample!

The next day we drove the precious cargo the twenty-minute drive to the nearest lab. We had to drive like crazy people to get it there in time, because, of course, we hit every red light there was. We just made it under the wire—both of us completely stressed from all of this. Who would have thought that getting a semen sample would turn out to be such an ordeal!

On the way home we stopped at a store and ran into my brother Calvin. He opened my door of the vehicle to say hello and found me sitting there with tears streaming down my face. He looked at me with concern and quietly asked, "Why are you crying?" I answered through my tears, "We are trying to have a baby, and these people are making it so damn difficult."

After a couple more days of waiting, the results of the sperm test came out normal. Wes was fine.

Well, of course he would be—he already had a child. So the problem was with me. There was something "wrong with me"! Again, I heard that echo in my head.

My family doctor referred me to a specialist, where a series of tests showed I had a blockage in my tubes. I underwent a minor procedure to have the blockage removed. After the requisite two weeks to heal, Wes and I said to each other, "Okay, we're good now; let's make a baby!" And we had fun trying!

But my biological clock continued to click. Time went on. And two years later, I still was not pregnant.

Dreams Derailed

One morning I woke up after sleeping on my stomach and noticed a strange feeling in my lower abdomen, as if I had been lying on a golf ball. I thought there must be something in the bed, but there wasn't. I then put my hand on my abdomen and felt a rather large lump in my stomach.

Off to the doctor I went again and had an ultrasound done. A couple of days later she called and asked me to come to her office. Now I was worried! Sitting in her office, she looked at me with concern and said, "You need to have emergency surgery. There is a lump on your ovary, and it is suspicious for cancer." My heart fell into my stomach. Those are the words everyone dreads hearing from their doctor.

I was booked for surgery a week later—the longest week of my life. I didn't want to say anything to anyone, even my parents, as I didn't want to worry them. I simply told them I was having exploratory surgery.

On the day of my surgery, my doctor came in and told me she would do everything she could to keep the ovary and my uterus intact, but if it was cancer, they would have to be removed. The ride on the gurney to the operating room was the scariest moment I have ever had in my life. Wes and Chris were both there walking along side of me. Wes kissed me and said, "See you later; I love you," as the doors to the OR closed between us.

When I woke up, Wes and Chris were sitting beside my bed, each holding one of my hands. Shortly thereafter, the doctor came in to tell us the verdict. She said, "You don't have cancer." An enormous relief went though my body. "You had a large fibroid the size of a grapefruit on your ovary, and I had to remove it . . . it also encompassed part of your uterus, and I had to remove it as well." I was still very groggy, and the news didn't sink in.

When the doctor left the room, two of my sisters and my mom, who had been waiting outside to see me, walked in. Wes told them the results of the surgery.

Wes and Christopher were still standing beside my bed, holding my hands. I looked up at Christopher; he looked so afraid. He was only about ten years old, and he hadn't seen anyone in the hospital before. He knew I was sick, but he didn't really understand what was going on.

What do you say to a child who doesn't understand when your heart is breaking? How do you hold it together for someone else when you are falling apart inside? I just took his hand and pulled it to my mouth and kissed it. I said to him, "Don't worry, I'll be okay, but I guess we won't be having anymore babies; you will be our only one." Chris leaned down and quietly said in my ear, "I love you." Those were the only words he spoke. I looked at him and said, "I love you too!"

My two sisters suddenly left the room. I didn't realize until later that they both were crying and didn't want me to see. Their hearts were breaking for me too.

Later in the evening, once the anesthetic wore off, lying alone in my room, it didn't take long for it to sink in: my dreams of having children had been shattered. My whole world was turned upside down.

In the days following my surgery, I grew more and more depressed. My recovery was a very slow one. Physically my body was healing normally, but mentally and emotionally . . . I would never fully recover.

Again, I felt inadequate as a woman. I talked to Wes about it, but he didn't feel it as deeply as I did; he had a son. We talked about adoption, but by this time I was already thirty-seven years old. We both had heard the horror stories about the length of time it takes to go through the adoption process, and with all the screening and red tape, we just didn't want to face all that.

We also talked about in vitro fertilization. But we knew how expensive it was, and we didn't have the money to pursue that option either. Two of my nieces, Jodie and Charlene, offered to be surrogate mothers for us. If we hadn't had Christopher, we might have considered this option, but Christopher was now living with us full time. On the surface, I was happy just having him in our lives and having our turn at being full-time parents. This lessened the pain a little.

Rage and Mourning

But inside I was angry. I was mad at the world and everyone in it, and especially angry at God! Everyday I saw women around me having babies. I would have made a wonderful mother and God didn't give me that chance. Well, screw God and everyone else too!

For years I avoided attending baby showers or being around young babies. It deeply hurt sitting around, seeing everyone goo and gawk over the baby and the cute little clothes. The women would all share their pregnancy stories, and they all thought theirs was the worst pregnancy or delivery in the entire history of motherhood. One woman told me how terrible her pregnancy was, and all I could say was, "I would have just liked being pregnant."

I would never be able to experience pregnancy, giving birth, hearing my child cry for the first time or say the word "Mommy." I didn't want to be around expectant mothers. Why did they get to have a child and not I? I constantly mourned for the child I would never have.

One night, on the evening news, I heard about a young teenage girl who had thrown her baby into a dumpster shortly after giving birth. I was shocked! How could someone do this? How could someone throw away a baby they had been blessed with? I was livid! The next day I submitted the following letter to the editor of the *Edmonton Journal*:

"This letter is addressed to the young woman who threw her baby away in a dumpster. I can only imagine how you are feeling, and I am sure you are very frightened and confused. Maybe you felt you were all alone and could not care for your child. Maybe you were too afraid to tell your parents. I hope you will seek professional help.

Now I would like you to imagine how I feel. I am a thirty-seven year old woman. I am married to a very loving and supportive man, and because we were in our thirties we decided to start a family. After two years we had no success. I had to get an operation to repair my tubes and still nothing. I finally ended up having to have a hysterectomy, ending any hope of having a baby.

I now distance myself from babies and pregnant women. I block out conversations of other women talking about their pregnancies and childbirth experiences. I do not attend baby showers and no longer hold other people's babies because it is too painful and I am afraid of breaking down.

Luckily I have a wonderful stepson whom I think of as my own. This helps to ease the pain.

So to you, and to any other young mothers in the future who are thinking of throwing your baby away, think of me. I will gladly take your baby."

If you have ever had a broken heart, you will understand how I felt. My heart had been pulled from my chest and ripped in two. I can only imagine, but to me, the only thing worse than not being able to have a child would be to lose one.

CHAPTER 4

DEPRESSION HURTS

*When you find yourself cocooned in isolation
and cannot find your way out of the darkness,
Remember that this is similar to the place
where caterpillars go to grow their wings.*

~Unknown

My depression grew deeper and deeper as time went on. I missed work, I stayed in bed all day, and I cried. I cried at breakfast, lunch, and dinner. I cried in the kitchen, in the bedroom, or in the basement. I shouted at Wes and Chris for every little thing—they couldn't do anything right. I was in a black cloud of doom and gloom, and I couldn't find my way out.

Everything I did was a struggle. I wasn't interested in doing anything, I didn't go out, I didn't have friends, and I didn't want any. I didn't care how I looked. Even simple things like taking a shower or brushing my teeth were hard. I would lie on the couch and watch mindless TV.

And I ate. I'm only five feet tall, and I ate myself up to over 200 pounds.

The pain I felt in depression was worse than any physical pain I had ever felt. Wes did some reading about it, which gave him some idea of what I was going through. But nobody really understood. Even my mom asked me one day, "What do you have to be depressed about? You have a good job, a nice house, a wonderful husband and stepson." She could see only the good things in my life. She really didn't understand.

No one understood that I felt empty, alone, and numb. I felt nothing! I had no emotions whatsoever. I would almost have preferred to feel pain rather than nothing at all—at least then I would have felt alive. But I felt dead inside.

I went to psychologists, therapists, and psychiatrists. I tried this drug and that drug, with very little effect. One medication I loved, because it numbed me and I no longer felt the pain. But I was like a zombie. I would look at Wes with my eyes glazed over; he said it was as if I were looking right through him.

By this time we lived just outside of a small town on an acreage, with a dog that liked to run after vehicles. One day, as I was pulling out of the driveway to go to town for groceries, the dog ran at my tires and I accidentally ran over him. I didn't kill him, but he was so badly injured that Wes had to put him down. Christopher cried, Wes felt awful—and I had no emotion whatsoever. You would think that losing a family pet might have rattled something inside, but it didn't.

As the years passed, depression became my norm. I couldn't remember what being happy felt like anymore. I tried to put on a happy face when I was around other people, but I felt like such a phony.

I knew the depression wasn't affecting just me; it was affecting my family and everyone around me. I'd talk to Wes, my mom, and sisters, trying to help them understand what I was going through. They'd listen and try to help but didn't know what to do. I knew they were all very concerned about me. My mom and dad were constantly asking me, "Are you okay?"

I could feel Wes and me starting to drift apart. He spent more and more time with his buddies in the garage, and I didn't care. I just wanted to be left alone. I didn't blame him for not wanting to be around me. Who would? He was so patient with me—my moods, tantrums, and outbursts. The man was a saint!

But I asked myself over and over again, "Is this all there is? Will I have to live like this for the rest of my life?"

I wanted to die!

CHAPTER 5

THE EASY WAY OUT

The hour of departure has arrived and we go our ways;
I to die, and you to live. Which is better? Only God knows.

~Socrates

Around the same time I was going through my depression, my sister Koreen was going through a hell of her own. Her youngest son, BJ, now in his late teens, was also having issues with depression. His best friend, Kevin, had recently committed suicide.

Late one night as Koreen was sleeping, she was awakened by a loud noise coming from BJ's bedroom. Warn, her husband, was working out of town, and she was alone with her kids. She ran downstairs to see what the noise was. She tried to open BJ's bedroom door but wasn't able to, as something was blocking it.

She knew something was very wrong. She frantically called to her daughter Charlene to come and help. When they were able to open the door enough to get into the room, they found BJ slumped against the door with a rope around his neck. He had tried to hang himself, but the rope had broken. Thank God he was still alive! He was rushed to the hospital and spent several days unconscious in Intensive Care.

When Warn and Koreen took BJ home from the hospital, they would not let him out of their sight. They didn't sleep; their lives literally robbed from them as they did everything they could to get help for their son.

Once BJ recovered from the attempt, we had a family meeting. Koreen wanted all of us to tell BJ how what he'd done had affected us, in hopes it would rid him of suicidal thoughts. We all told him how much we loved him, and how he had scared us. Some even confessed they were angry for him having put us through the possibility of losing him. He promised us it wouldn't happen again.

But several months later, I had just gotten home from work when my dad called. He rarely called me—my mom was the one who did the calling—so I knew immediately something was wrong. "Carla, I have some very bad news," he said. "BJ is gone."

"Oh my God!" I cried. I couldn't believe it. He had finally done what we all had feared. What I had thought about doing so many times.

Wes and I headed to Edmonton to Koreen and Warn's house. BJ's body was still in the basement. He had used a shotgun, and Koreen had found him when she got home from work. By the time we arrived, the house was filled with police, social workers, and the coroner. We all watched as they removed his body on a stretcher and placed it in an unmarked van.

A couple of hours later, I remember looking at my sister. She was crying, and had been talking quietly about what happened. I saw the pain in her eyes. She was sitting in a chair, and I went up behind her and wrapped my arms around her. At that moment she cried out—I think the realization had just hit her—"OH MY GOD! I have lost my baby!"

Those words stung my ears. I held her with all the love and strength and support I could give and could feel her body tremble in my arms as she cried. I wanted so much to be able to take her pain away, but I couldn't.

There was a lot of commotion after that. Lots of people arrived to support Warn and Koreen. Fruit baskets and flower bouquets arrived by the dozens. Trays of food and sandwiches were donated by caring neighbours. Warn and Koreen, and her ex-husband George, had lost their son. Devlon, Geordie, and Charlene had lost their brother. He was only nineteen years old.

The day before the funeral, my mom and dad came to my house for a visit. Dad was sitting silently outside by the picnic table. I was puttering around watering flowers. He called me over and looked into my eyes and asked me if I was okay. I could see the look of concern and worry in his eyes. Without him saying anything, I knew what he was thinking. He did not want to have to go through what my sister and her family had just been through.

I assured him I was okay and made a silent promise to him that I would not put him or my family through that pain again. The stress and anxiety on my sister and her family were physically visible. She had aged ten years in a matter of months while dealing with BJ's threats of suicide and his eventual death.

Koreen returned to work a couple of weeks after the funeral. I thought it was too soon, but she insisted she needed something to occupy her mind. Soon after, she started volunteering for Victim Services. After only a few months we noticed a difference in her. The depression she had felt seemed to be fading away. She seemed less anxious and more at peace. When we asked her how she was doing, she said, "I'm doing okay. I have three other children I need to live for."

After BJ's death I did everything I could to find answers and relief for my depression. At one time I had thought that suicide might be an easy way out to end the misery I was feeling, but I now knew it was not an option. I couldn't put my family through that. I needed to find a solution and I wouldn't give up until I did.

My nephew BJ had saved my life

CHAPTER 6

OUR GOOD SON

*Rock bottom became the solid foundation
on which I built my life.*

~J.K. Rowling

Christopher was ten years old when he came to live with us full-time. He had always been reserved and quiet. He was well-behaved, respectful, and never talked back. People constantly complimented us on what a good boy we had.

At first, living together was a huge adjustment for all three of us. I was used to being able to come and go as I pleased. I wasn't used to having a young boy around, and I often lost my patience with him. I would scream and yell, then feel very bad afterward, hugging him and telling him, "I'm so sorry."

I went through the motions of trying to be a good mother to Chris; after all, he was the only son I would ever know. I smothered him with motherly affections, wanting him to love me as if I were his real mother—who lived two thousand miles away on the East Coast. He didn't see her much, and, while I wasn't trying to replace her, I wanted him to feel loved.

I did all the things moms do, like going to his school functions and parent-teacher interviews. I was also a hockey mom and wouldn't miss a game. It was very hard for me to love anyone back then, but I tried to give him as much love as I could—and I did love Christopher as if he were my own.

After a few months we began to adjust and started to meld as a family. The longer Chris was with us, the closer we became. Then Chris grew into a teenager. He started going to parties, and we'd allow him to have parties at our house. We preferred for him to party at home than not know where he was. We talked to him about the dangers of drugs and alcohol, preached to him about drinking and driving—all the things parents warn their kids about. We hoped he was listening to us.

One night when he was about sixteen, he wanted to go to a friend's house. It was a weeknight, and he had to work the next day. (Chris was in an apprenticeship program where he worked and got credits for it in school.) "Well, okay, but don't be too late, you have to work tomorrow," I said. "Yeah, yeah, yeah," he said, mocking me with a grin on his face.

It got really late and Chris still wasn't home. This was back in 2002, when teenagers didn't carry cell phones—at least, not our teenager—so we had no way of getting in touch with him. I had gone to bed but couldn't sleep—I never slept much when he was out—so I got up and started pacing, watching the time tick slowly by. I finally lay on the couch, tossing, turning, waiting. By 3:00 a.m. he still wasn't home.

At 5:30 Wes got up for work, and when he came down to the living room, asked, "What are you doing down here?"

"Waiting for Chris; he's still not home," I said. I was sick with worry by this time. "Well, f—!" Wes exploded. He and Chris worked and drove together, and Wes paced around the kitchen, pissed off that his son was going to make him late for work.

Not long after, Chris pulled into the driveway. As he walked in the house, we immediately knew something was wrong. "Are you drunk?" Wes asked.

"No," Chris answered. But he was acting really strange. We had seen him drunk before, and it had been nothing like this. Then he started saying really strange things, telling us all the signs on the highway had been turned around and he couldn't find his way home. We knew he wasn't drunk. He was on something much stronger.

Wes and I were both panicked. I thought to myself, *Oh my God, he drove home like this.* So many scenarios of everything that could have happened to him or to other people on the road went through my mind. "What are you on Chris?" I asked him. He knew we knew he was on something, and he wasn't about to lie. "Speed," he said.

We took him to the hospital, as we didn't know what else to do. For several hours, Chris lay sleeping in a hospital bed, twitching and turning with an IV in his arm to wean him off the drugs.

The effects of the drugs were still present when we brought him home, so we didn't say much to him. After a long sleep, he got up. We sat down and had a long family discussion. We didn't reprimand him, we just talked. We asked him why he was doing drugs, telling him how they could ruin his life, and also told him we loved him very much. We told him everyone makes mistakes, and we hoped he had learned something from this.

Wake-Up Call

As time went on, things seemed to settle down. We believed the incident had scared him enough that he wouldn't do it again.

When he was eighteen years old, Chris moved out of the house and moved to Edmonton. He had a job there, some of his friends were there, and it was time for him to spread his wings. "Whoo-hoo! Time to put in the hot tub," we joked with him. We thought, "Great, he's grown up and moved out, and our job as parents is over." We soon came to realize, however, that our job as parents is never over.

One night shortly after Chris moved out, Wes came home from work and said, "Chris didn't show up for work today. He never called in to say he was sick." This concerned us because Chris never missed work. He worked with his dad and knew he would have to answer to him if he didn't show up. We tried calling him but received no response. We were worried, thinking he might be sick.

The next day I called Wes at work to see if Chris had shown up. "Nope," was his reply. "No phone call either?" I asked. "Nope." He was angry, but I could hear the sound of worry in his voice too. We were both worried.

Wes drove to Chris' house, about an hour away, after work, but there was no answer at the door. When he didn't show up for work for three days without calling, and our attempts to reach him were futile, through my tears I phoned the police and reported him as a missing person. The police officer said, "He's nineteen years old; there's really nothing we can do. He's probably out partying somewhere." I slammed the phone down in his ear, and my heart sank to the depths of my stomach.

We didn't hear from Chris for two long, agonizing weeks. We were frantic. We called all of his friends; they told us they hadn't seen him. We finally called one friend we knew was into the drug scene. We told him, "Tell Chris to call us immediately, or we're going to send the police to his house."

Chris called us the next day. "I'm sorry to have worried you, but I'm okay," he said. He told us he was stressed out from his job and needed to take a break. "What are you stressed about?" we asked, but he didn't have an answer for us. We knew our son was in big trouble.

A few months went by and we rarely heard from him. We didn't want to watch the evening news because we were afraid we would see our son there on the screen—in trouble. We made many attempts to reach him, but he wouldn't answer our calls. We'd even call from unfamiliar phone numbers, but as soon as he heard our voice he'd hang up. We then eliminated even the hello and would quickly say, "We love you, Chris," before he hung up, or "Chris, let us help you," before hearing the click.

Wes and I did a lot of drinking then—or maybe I was doing all the drinking. I needed something to numb the pain, worry, and fear I felt. I just couldn't bear the thought of losing the only son I had ever known. I know Wes felt the same. For the first time in both our lives, we started praying.

I can remember praying, *God, please take care of Chris* so many times, and yes, I admit, I even remember asking, *Please, Lord, stop him; have him get caught and taken to jail if that's what it takes.* I knew it might be the one thing that could stop him from the deadly lifestyle he was living. What kind of mother prays for her son to go to jail?

Our prayers were answered. He did get caught, and he did go to jail, and it was only then that he called us for help. *Thank you, God.*

He was placed in the Edmonton Remand Centre for ten days. We went to visit him only once while he was incarcerated; it was a very scary place even to visit. He was brought into a little cubicle, looking thin, disheveled, wearing blue coveralls. We hadn't seen him in months. Plexiglas separated us from him, so we couldn't hug him or touch him. We had to speak to him through a phone receiver.

I picked up the phone and said to him "Chris, we love you and we will do anything and everything we can to get you out of here, but you have to change your lifestyle. We cannot support you if you continue to live the way you have been living."

It was tough love, but we knew in our hearts that this might be our only chance of getting him back. Wes and I had written up a contract and read it to him with the conditions he would have to follow to get out. He was not allowed to have contact with the people he had been hanging out with, he would have to move back home, he would have to go back to work, and absolutely no drugs were allowed. He agreed to our terms, so we bailed him out of jail.

The first time he had to appear in court before he was released, they brought him into the courtroom. There he was, our well-behaved boy, respected and loved by all who knew him—in handcuffs and shackles. He was like a different person. Someone we had never met. He glimpsed our way and saw we were there, but quickly turned away. He couldn't face us.

But we would not and did not give up on him. We knew our good boy was in there somewhere and we needed to find him again.

After thousands of dollars in legal fees and several court appearances, he was placed on house arrest for one year. We brought our son home, put our lives on hold, and focused on healing him and our relationship with him. We spent all of our time with him. We played cards and games as a family. Wes spent hours in the garage with him. We told him how much we loved him, and we supported him as much as we knew how.

Amazingly, going to jail saved his life, going to jail saved our relationship with him, and going to jail was the thing he needed to turn his life around.

It was Chris who made me realize how precious life is. We almost lost him, but luckily we got him back. He made me realize how short life is and made me want to live life to the fullest, to make good and healthy choices in my own life. He made me realize how important love is, and that when you don't give up, good things do come out of it.

Maybe there really was a God after all . . .

PART II

THE TURNING POINT

With my last breath, I'll exhale my love for you.
I hope it's a cold day, so you can see what you meant to me.

~Jarod Kintz

CHAPTER 7

FAREWELL PARTY

I t was now October 2002. I was at work when I got the call from my mom. Dad had just been to the doctor. My dad was not a healthy man for the last five years of his life. He had a lung condition that required him to be hooked up to oxygen twenty-four hours a day, and lately his symptoms seemed to be getting worse. "Carla," my mom said, "the doctor found a spot on your dad's lungs, and he needs to have a biopsy."

I left work immediately. I knew this was not good. When I got there I tried to be positive. I gave him a big hug, and he said, "Don't worry, I'm going to fight this." He was a stubborn man, my dad, so this comforted me . . . a little.

The results of his biopsy a couple days later were what we had all feared: he had a very aggressive form of lung cancer. I remember sitting at the hospital with him, my mom, and most of my brothers and sisters when he got the news. The doctor said, "I'm sorry, but you don't have long to live. We can do treatment, which will give you six months, maybe, and without treatment, six weeks."

I drove my mom and dad home that day. In silence, I held my dad's hand the entire way home. He had big, strong, rough hands, and to me it was the most comforting thing. Even now I really miss holding his hand.

Over the next couple of days my mom and dad had a lot of decisions to make, but Dad decided he was not going to go for treatment. "Why prolong the inevitable and the suffering?" he said.

I spent time with my dad every day after that, stopping in after work to visit. I was grateful to live only a few minutes away. I could see the difference in him every day and how quickly he was deteriorating.

Dad hadn't slept in a bed for the last thirty years of his life. He said it was hard for him to breathe, and his back would get sore lying down. So he always slept sitting up on his favorite place on the couch in the living room. When he got sick, we brought in a hospital bed, and placed it in the living room, thinking it would be more comfortable for him. But he never used it, so instead, my mom slept there to be near him.

People came to visit him throughout the day, and we kids watched over him throughout the night. It was busy, noisy, and hectic with so many people coming and going all the time.

But my dad's wish was to die at home. He did not want to die in a hospital, and we did everything we could to grant him his last wish. We had home care come in to give him his meds, and for the last two weeks all eight of us took shifts to care for him round the clock. The home care nurses inserted a catheter type device in his chest, which allowed us to give him his pain medicine with a syringe.

On one particular day, a home care nurse came in and started to cry. She said, "I have never seen so much love and caring in a family before. I have seen many people die alone; you are truly blessed!"

It is a good thing we were blessed with so many kids in our family. It was difficult as it was, and would have been even more difficult if the numbers had been smaller. Two or three of us were on constant care duty. We'd take three- or four-hour shifts, keeping close watch on him and giving him his meds when home care wasn't on duty. We would rub his back and his feet, and look after his every need. It was during these times, very late at night, or in the wee hours of the morning, when we would sit, play cards, reminisce about old times, or just talk quietly that we were brought even closer as a family. It was stressful, it was tiring, and it was draining, but it was also very special.

I went home one night after a long shift and decided to have a bath to help me relax so I could sleep. I climbed into the bathtub; the hot water pierced my skin. I lay back. It was at that moment, while soaking in the tub, I realized my dad was really dying. I screamed out, "Oh my God, my dad is dying!" I cried harder than I had cried in my entire life.

At this point my dad was hooked up to an IV, as he could no longer eat solid food. He had a urinary catheter, and he slept most of the time. He could no longer speak. His lips were cracked and dry, so we gave him ice chips to suck on to help keep him hydrated. Dad loved sweets, so one day I went to the store and bought him a popsicle and fed it to him when I got back. He completely devoured it in seconds. Without saying anything, he reached out and gave me the biggest hug. I cried.

Over the next few days he rapidly deteriorated. He was visibly losing weight and lost consciousness. The only way we knew he was still with us was the purring sound of the oxygen machine every time he took a breath. Most of the family was there now, his sister and brother, we kids, and a lot of his grandchildren. Not knowing if he could hear us, we sat around him telling stories, laughing, and taking turns telling him what he meant to us, what our favorite times with him had been, and how much we loved him.

During one of these times, after being unconscious for several days, without opening his eyes or moving at all, he just softly spoke the words "Thank you!" We all hugged him and each other and cried.

One day, Dad woke up and asked my mom, "Where's Dad and Albert?" His dad and his brother Albert had passed several years before. He became very agitated, sat straight up and said, "Thank you all for everything you've done; I've had enough of this; I have to go"—and started ripping his IV out of his arm. We quickly settled him down again and he fell back into unconsciousness.

As I mentioned previously, my family is very musical, and we got this from our dad. He loved music. One Saturday night we got the guitars out and started singing, playing all his favorite tunes. It wasn't long into this music session that my sister Kim pointed at Dad and shouted, "Look, Dad is tapping his toe." Sure enough, ever so slightly we could see his toe tapping in time to the music. We smiled and we laughed.

The next day, Sunday morning, five weeks after his diagnosis, my mom and four of us girls were keeping busy cleaning the house and doing some chores. My brothers had gone to the airport to pick up more family members. With just the five of us it was very quiet and peaceful, compared to the full house we were used to.

While we were busying ourselves and puttering around, my sister Phyllis sat down with Dad. A few minutes later she yelled, "Mom! He stopped breathing!" We all ran over to him. Two of my sisters sat beside him, my mom knelt between his knees, and I knelt down beside her. We knew he was gone, that he had chosen this quiet time, when few people were around. My mom wrapped her arms around him, I took his arms and wrapped them around her, and at that moment, he took one last breath for her. I looked at his face, and I saw one tear in the corner of his eye.

We all sat there holding him, hugging each other, and crying for a long time. Someone, I'm not sure who, unplugged the oxygen machine, and for once in a very long time, there was complete silence . . . and peace.

The next few days were very hectic, contacting people and planning a funeral. The evening before the funeral, we were all sitting around what was once again the living room, instead of the makeshift hospital room it had been the last five weeks. Mom and Dad had a clock on the TV, and all of a sudden the alarm on this clock went off. Even though it had been sitting there for years the alarm had never been set. In our hearts, we knew it was Dad letting us know he was there with us and okay! We cried.

My dad was not a religious man. Any religion I had growing up came from my mom. My dad did not want to have a funeral, but we decided we needed one for us. We didn't want a lot of Bible readings and praying—just music. So some of his friends played instruments and, other than the eulogy and the Lord's Prayer, the entire ceremony was music. All of us kids sang his favorite hymn.

One of my dad's favorite songs was called "Farewell Party." My nephew Geordie played guitar and, with tears flowing down his cheeks, he sang "Farewell Party," performing one last time for Grandpa.

And that is exactly what we did! After the funeral, we had a party! We celebrated his life. We drank, we laughed, we sang, we played guitars, we danced, and we all knew Dad was there and smiling down on us.

It has been ten years since Dad's passing. Before that day I never would have thought of it as "passing." I would have referred to it as death, as being gone forever. But it was that day and the weeks leading up to it and afterward that started me on a spiritual journey that has changed my life completely.

Before this, I never would have considered death to be beautiful. Don't get me wrong—it was a very sad time for me. I was angry, I was afraid; the family I had known all my life was about to change dramatically. But it would be a turning point for me, nonetheless.

Even ten years later as I write this, I remember every single detail as if it were yesterday, which seems funny because I can't remember much about my life ten years ago, I was living in such a fog.

We had another sign of Dad's presence later. The summer after he died, most of the family attended a live country music festival. On Saturday afternoon we decided we were all going to see the next performer. Once we were all together and settled in our seats, the band started to play their next song. As soon as the first three or four bars were played, we looked at each other, recognizing the familiar notes from "Farewell Party." Because this isn't a very well-known song, we knew our dad was with us then too.

During the time of his illness, the time of sadness, grief, and pain, the time I thought was the worst time in my life, I found God. There was so much love in that house, God's presence was felt everywhere. I received so many gifts from that experience: love, hope, faith, a closeness with my family that is very rare, and beautiful memories I will treasure for the rest of my life.

My dad's passing was the shift I needed that started me on a spiritual journey that has been nothing short of a miracle. I used to be afraid of death and dying. But I'm no longer afraid, as I know without a doubt only our bodies die; our spirits live on forever.

When the last breath of life is gone from my body,
and my lips are as cold as the sea
When my friends gather round for my farewell party
Won't you please say you'll love me

I hope you'll have fun at my farewell party
Please don't be sad when I'm gone.[1]

Thank you, Dad for all the love and support you gave me. I love you—and I'll see you at the party!

---

[1] Lyrics from "Farewell Party," recorded in 1979 by Gene Watson.

CHAPTER 8

WAIT! IT'S NOT ABOUT THE WEIGHT

*Being thin does not address the emptiness
that has no shape or weight or name.
Even a wildly successful diet is a colossal failure because
inside the new body is the same sinking heart.*

~Geneen Roth

I have always had issues with food. I have never been a person to eat when I was hungry and stop when I was full; food has been an obsession. I never had a weight problem growing up, because I was more on the anorexic side; I managed my fears of getting fat by eating only one meal a day. I've heard many overweight women say they didn't have a weight problem until they had kids. Well, my excuse was *not* having kids.

With all the stress and disappointments life had dealt me—depression, infertility, death, worrying about Chris—I was eating my way into oblivion. I now weighed 226 pounds, falling into the majorly obese category for my height of five feet. I had tried several times and several different diets to lose the weight, but to no avail. I'd do well for a few days, then get into a slump and binge my way back to where I'd been before.

I was addicted to food. I couldn't stop eating. Food was like a drug, and I was using it to fill the emptiness I felt in my heart. I felt disgusted when I looked in the mirror, and I hated the person looking back at me. One evening I found myself praying, *Please God, please help me stop eating.*

About a month later I was at a meeting at work and saw a woman I hadn't seen in a few months. She looked absolutely amazing! I say this because she had gone from being obese to a normal weight. She was glowing, beautiful, and happy. I pulled her aside and said, "I want what you have. Tell me what you did!"

She proceeded to tell me about a program she was doing, based on the same concept as Alcoholics Anonymous, but a twelve-step program to help food addicts lose weight. She explained that I would have to give up eating flour and sugar—and no alcohol was allowed.

My first thought was, *Well, not sure I can do that.* Then I heard a voice in my head say, "If you want to help Chris with his addiction, you need to get control of your own."

So for the next meeting to be held in my area, I drove an hour and a half to Red Deer to check it out. My first meeting was a little scary, but after attending a couple, it felt like a safe place, and I thought I'd give it a try. I could share with others all the things I had gone through—and they would listen.

Like Alcoholics Anonymous, this program was based on the premise that we need to find our higher power, and that this higher power would help us get through each day, each hour, and each minute so we would not have to resort to eating anything other than the strict meal plan we were given. It required us to sit quietly or meditate for half an hour a day. That is when meditation was introduced into my life.

Over the next eleven months I cut out all flour, sugar, and alcohol from my diet. I ate healthy food and exercised. I started running, weight training, and doing yoga, which enabled me to lose almost one hundred pounds. I was healthy, and I felt great physically.

People commented on how great I looked. It was a little embarrassing for me at first, because I was used to hiding in the corner trying to be invisible so people wouldn't see how fat I was. I was used to feeling like a "nobody" and that I didn't matter. Now people were paying attention, and it was uncomfortable. I didn't know how to take it.

It was uncomfortable for Wes too. He told me that he was jealous of all the attention I was getting.

Before I lost my weight, I always felt that if I could just be slim, I would feel better about myself and I wouldn't be depressed anymore. Life would be wonderful.

But that didn't happen. Now I was slimmer than I'd been in high school. Physically I felt sexy and beautiful. But mentally, I still felt depressed and miserable. I still did not like the person in this thin, healthy body.

After so many years of not loving or even liking who I was, I realized my scars were not on the surface, but much deeper. I needed to find a way to love myself again.

CHAPTER 9

HAPPINESS LIES WITHIN

Realize that true happiness lies within you.
Remember that there is no happiness in having or getting,
but only in giving.

~Og Mandino

I began reading many spiritual books to try and heal my soul. My meditation sessions were starting to become a habit and a comfort for me as well. I'd often think of all the things that made me miserable: I couldn't have a baby, my job was stressful, we were always broke, my dad and BJ had died, we had gone through so much trouble with Chris, my husband didn't do his part in making me happy . . . blah, blah, blah. I blamed everyone and everything for my unhappiness.

Then, during one of my meditation sessions, I heard a voice say loud and clear, "No one or nothing can make you happy. Your happiness is inside you. It comes from within."

My eyes bolted open! Wow! This was a real "aha" moment, but it was more than that to me. It was as if a baseball bat had just hit me over the head. All this time I had been blaming my husband, my son, and my job for my rotten life—and all of it was my own doing!

This became even more evident to me while working on a very stressful computer system implementation at work. After weeks of trying to figure out a problem we were having, we found the solution. "Yes!" We were all overjoyed to have figured it out. As I walked out of my office to make a copy of something, I overheard one of my co-workers saying, "Wow, that is the first time I have ever seen Carla smile." She had been working there almost a year. I stopped in my tracks and thought, *Wow, am I really that bad?* It was at that moment I made the choice to become happy.

One day, shortly after, I was watching "Oprah" on TV. They were advertising the next day's airing and said, "Don't miss tomorrow's show. If you want to know the secret to happiness, fulfillment, to life, then tune in tomorrow." I was really intrigued.

The next day after work I made a point to get home in time to watch "Oprah." I felt a sense of urgency to see this show. But it was the middle of winter, and the roads were snow covered and icy. I was driving a little faster than I should have been for the road conditions, and suddenly my vehicle started spinning out of control and I hit the ditch.

"SHIT! I'm going to miss Oprah!" That's all I could think about. I tried to back my truck out, but, sure enough, I was stuck. I called home, and Wes and Chris came and pulled me out of the ditch.

I made it home in time to see the last half hour of the show. They were talking about a new movie called *The Secret*, which was becoming something of a phenomenon. Rhonda Byrne, director of the movie, was explaining how there is a universal energy that we all have access to. That this energy is in all of us. That we create our own lives. That everything begins with a thought, and it's our thoughts that create our reality.

She explained what is known as the "Law of Attraction." When you think positive thoughts, you attract positive things into your life. When you think about negative things, then negative things are attracted to you.

At that moment I said, "OH MY GOD!" Another aha moment! But this one was huge, even bigger than the previous one.

I looked back at my life and everything that had happened over the last few years. All of my thoughts had been negative. All I ever thought about was how rotten my life was.

I immediately went online and ordered the movie. I could hardly wait to watch it. I felt all the answers to all the questions I had had all my life would be on that DVD. I felt it and I knew it.

The day it arrived, I waited all night for Wes and Chris to go to bed. Intuitively I knew this was my personal journey and I needed to take it alone. Once they went to bed, I plugged it into the DVD player.

In *The Secret*, Neale Donald Walsch said, "There is no chalk board in the sky that says (your name)'s purpose is (fill in the blank)." I had always wondered what my purpose was. Now I suddenly realized that my purpose was to live my best life and be the best person I could be. It didn't mean I needed to be famous, and it didn't mean I needed to be rich. But I got that as long as we are following our passions and sharing our gifts with others, we will be rewarded. That is our purpose!

I started bawling my eyes out. I knew God or the Universe didn't expect me to do great things and change the world; all he wanted was for me to be happy and live life on my terms and no one else's. Whatever it is that makes me happy—that is what I was put here to do.

After watching *The Secret*, everything made so much sense to me. It was as if my life and everything that had happened was so clear to me. Every piece of the puzzle began falling into place. Every time I needed something, it showed up in my life.

I also remember reading Wayne Dyer's book *The Power of Intention*, where he said we can have anything we choose to have, we just need to set an intention, visualize it in our minds, and it will unfold.

I realized this is exactly what I had done with Chris. I had prayed so hard every day for him to get caught and go to jail. I had prayed for him to come home, and I had imagined us being a happy family again. I had kept the vision in my head and played it over and over and over again—and that is exactly how it happened.

I realized the Universe had brought the weight-loss program to me when I had asked for it, at the exact perfect time I was ready and able to commit to it.

I also realized the reason I couldn't have children: I needed to be a mother to Chris. I needed to support him and love him through his drug addiction.

CHAPTER 10

ADDICTED TO
HAPPINESS

When you are clear, what you want
will show up in your life—
and only to the extent that you are clear.

~Janet Attwood

Over the next two years I studied many of the teachers in *The Secret*, including Bob Proctor, Neale Donald Walsch, Bill Harris, Jack Canfield—all of them. My thirst and hunger for this knowledge was insatiable. I couldn't get enough of it, and I felt happier by the minute. I had been able to put down the food, but this was my new addiction. Surely it couldn't be wrong to be addicted to happiness, could it?

I was on top of the world. I had a warmth in my heart I had never felt before. I finally knew what happiness felt like, and I shared it with everyone I knew.

I seemed to attract every personal development course on the planet, and I attended every one I possibly could. I was challenged to do things I never dreamed I was capable of. I walked on fire, broke arrows with my throat, and met and spent time with many successful, well-known, and influential people.

I went to Florida and studied for a week with Bob Proctor, becoming a Certified LifeSuccess Consultant; I was now able to teach his programs to others. My sister Phyllis also studied with me, and together we formed a business that we shared with our family and our friends. I could see the difference it was making in their lives too.

I went to Toronto and spent three days with Chris Attwood and Janet Bray Attwood, *New York Times* bestselling authors of *The Passion Test*. I became a Passion Test Facilitator. I was passionate about inspiring others to find their passions, so they could live purposeful, happy lives like I was now living.

I had let go of my resentments, come to terms with being childless, and was now accepting and happy with the person I was for the first time in my life. I was falling in love with my life and myself.

Chris was home and doing well. He had been clean for three years and was now a journeyman in his trade. He was making good money. He was responsible and, in my eyes, the most amazing person in the world. I was so incredibly proud of him for all he had accomplished, and I told him so constantly.

My job was so much better. I didn't feel stressed out anymore like I used to; in fact, I was actually starting to enjoy it.

I no longer worried about anything. I knew that everything happens for a reason and turns out exactly as it should. I was much less critical of others, realizing that they too were on a journey and choosing to have the experiences they were having.

I was happy—heck, even ecstatic. But there was still one thing that kept gnawing at me. It was like a knot in my stomach, and I had felt it for a very long time.

My intuition was telling me something still wasn't right.

CHAPTER 11

ANOTHER
BROKEN HEART

In the process of letting go,
you will lose many things from the past,
but you will find yourself.

~Deepak Chopra

W es was working away from home and only came home on weekends. This gave me time to pursue my LifeSuccess and Passion Test businesses.

When he did come home, it seemed he still spent much of his weekends in the garage. And even when he was home, I felt alone. I told him, "Wes, you need to spend more time with your wife."

For a long time I had been questioning where our marriage was going. In the beginning I had loved him more than anything in the world. He was a wonderful husband to me. He had supported me in everything. He had put up with my moods. He had treated me with kid gloves because of my depression. He didn't understand it, but he had stood by me and did all he could to try to make me happy. My family loved him and he fit in really well with them.

For the first seven years of our marriage, we had communicated well and were very close. After that, something changed. Our primary focus became raising our son, and our relationship came second.

During the time Chris was going through his ordeal, Wes and I seemed to get closer again. We comforted each other, because all we had was each other.

Then when Chris came home and was on house arrest for that year, we put our lives on hold. We didn't go anywhere. We chose to stay home so that we could support him and heal our relationship with him. We spent hours playing cards and games. Wes and Chris spent a lot of time in the garage building an all-terrain dune buggy from the ground up. It was all great therapy for Chris.

It was during this time I started attending the personal growth seminars. I was changing, inside and out. I was leading mastermind groups with my family and friends, as well as running my own LifeSuccess and Passion Test workshops. I preached to the attendees to live their dreams, that they could do anything they chose to do. I repeated over and over to them, "You are responsible for your own happiness," all the while feeling empty inside where my marriage was concerned.

I could see Wes and Chris becoming closer and closer, but I felt we were drifting further apart. I was growing in one direction and they were going in another. My life seemed to be taking a different path, and my interests were changing. I felt that Wes and I no longer had anything in common, and I no longer felt connected to him. I could still feel the knot in my stomach. It wouldn't go away, and it kept gnawing at me.

I mentioned to him several times that we were losing our connection and we needed to spend more time together. I asked him to go on a retreat with me, but he wasn't really crazy about doing it; that just wasn't his "thing."

I realized I needed to come to a decision: I either needed to work on my marriage and find what was missing, or I needed to leave.

It was the most difficult decision of my life. Growing up, it had been drilled into my head that marriage was a commitment; you make a vow, you keep it.

I knew if I did leave I was taking the risk of losing Chris. I was also taking the risk of not having the opportunity to be a grandmother to his children. I knew my family would be hurt and the friends we knew as a couple would change.

The battle went on in my head and my heart for many months. For a few weeks I'd be content—everything would be fine. Then for a few weeks I'd be restless. I just couldn't see myself staying in this rut. I wanted something much more, and I kept feeling this turmoil inside my body.

One Saturday, on one of his weekends home, Wes came into the house from the garage. He said, "Do you want to go out for supper?" I thought, *No I don't want to go out for supper. That's all we do to be together. We go out for supper, sit in silence, and then come home. Then you go back out to the garage and I sit here alone again in the house.* Writing this, I realize that I didn't say it out loud for him to hear. If I had, would it have made a difference?

I said, "No I don't want to go for supper. I can't do this anymore." He said, "Do what anymore?" with a scared look on his face. I said, "You and me, and our marriage." I said, "I love you, but I am no longer *in* love with you."

Immediately he started sobbing. He knew as well as I did it was over. He had felt it too; there was no point in carrying on. He was also tired of always trying to please me; he was tired of having to always try so hard to get me to love him. He deserved much more than what I could give him. And I had to learn to love myself again before I would be able to love anyone else.

With his heart breaking, and with a look of defeat on his face, he got up, grabbed his suitcase, still packed from his week away, and walked away.

My heart was also breaking. How could I do this to the man I had spent the last twenty years of my life with? How could I do this to my best friend?

Most of our friends took Wes's side; many in my family were angry with me and deeply hurt. They loved him very much.

I cried for the next three months. I questioned my decision over and over again. Had I done the right thing? I kept in close touch with Wes and Chris; I needed to make sure they were okay.

I felt guilty. Terrible. I felt like the most horrible person in the world. But I didn't want to go back. Even though it was difficult getting used to life on my own, I felt free. And I noticed the knot in my stomach disappeared.

Wes and I are still great friends, and I will love him till the day I die. I loved him enough to let him go, as he deserves someone who will love him unconditionally. He needed to be free to be the person he needs to be without having to worry if I was going to walk out on him all the time. I wasn't able to give him that. And we made the decision together that we didn't want our relationship to end in bitterness and anger, but in love.

Now, three years later, I know it was the right thing. I felt stifled there, and I never would have grown in the way that I have.

I needed to be me.

PART III

HEAVEN HERE
ON EARTH

When you do things from your soul
you feel a river moving in you . . . pure joy.

~Rumi

CHAPTER 12

LOSING MY RELIGION

After my divorce I did all I could to help myself heal and feel whole again—and to start living MY truth. I hungered for growth and wanted to devour anything that could help me develop myself.

Shortly after seeing the movie *The Secret*, I saw an ad in the local paper: Learn how to manifest everything you want, as in the movie *The Secret*. The ad was for a weekend-long seminar. I instantly signed up.

The course was called Theta Healing. During that weekend we were to learn how to clear any blocks preventing us from manifesting our desires. That we are all connected and share the same universal energy. And how we can connect with our creator and ask for what we want.

The group was all women, except for the man leading the course. In one session we were to ask a partner a question, then go into our meditative, or "theta state," and use universal energy to find the answer. It was my turn to answer the question for my partner. She asked, "Who is my spiritual guide?"

Now, the woman across from me, although I knew her name, was a total stranger. I closed my eyes and asked her spiritual guides to show themselves to me, not really believing they would. I started describing to her the visions coming into in my head. "Your spiritual guide is a man. He is dressed in a long, gray cloak; he has no hair; and he looks like a monk. He cares for you deeply. His name is Jake."

I heard the woman gasp, so I opened my eyes. She said, "That is amazing!" and started to cry. She proceeded to tell me that when she was a little girl, her dad had a friend, a very nice man who had always wanted to become a priest. He had passed away a few years before—and his name was Jake!

I was stunned! I couldn't believe what she was telling me. I had never had any such experiences prior to this.

This incident led me to believe even more that we really are all connected, and that tapping into a higher consciousness is possible—we just need to be open to it.

Wanting More

I was researching wellness retreats on the internet but hadn't found any that were affordable for me at the time. Then Phyllis and I went to an event that featured several speakers, one of whom was Satyan Raja, the founder of Warrior Sage. He was offering a weekend Illumination Intensive, which sounded exactly like what I was looking for. It was affordable and only a three-hour drive away.

I said to Phyllis, "I just manifested this. I have been looking for something like this, and the Universe just presented it to me." I immediately signed up.

Friday morning, March 27, 2009, I left on what I thought was going to be a meditation retreat. I was going on a relaxing weekend in the mountains, to return totally refreshed. I was so excited.

I headed down to Morley, Alberta, to the Nakoda Lodge nestled in a beautiful setting in the mountains. When I arrived, I had to turn in all of my personal belongings—purse, keys, and cell phone. All we were allowed to have with us were our clothes and toothbrush.

We were then instructed to settle into our rooms. There were four women to a room and, because I arrived early, I was lucky enough to get a bed, while two women who arrived later had to sleep on foamies on the floor.

Friday night was orientation. The staff were introduced and instructions on how the weekend would unfold were given. We were told the weekend would be very disciplined, in order for us to receive the most benefit. We reviewed all agreements: no makeup, jewelry, cell phones, music, books, etc.

There was also no caffeine allowed. One woman got very upset—she wanted her coffee! She left the seminar that night. We were told we would be eating a vegetarian diet of very small portions.

Late into the evening, we headed to bed with strict instructions to be silent. They'd knock on our doors in the morning; we had no idea what time morning meant, but knew it would be early. We would be given twenty minutes to be up and in the lodge, ready to start the day. *Twenty minutes for four women to get up and showered and ready to go—are you kidding me?* I thought. As it turned out, we didn't have time even to shower in the morning. We got up, got dressed, and brushed our hair and teeth—that was it.

The day began with a lecture and more instructions on how to do the "technique." This technique was going to help rid us of all the false ideas we had come to believe about ourselves. All the issues and beliefs we had buried deep inside that were holding us back from living a life we were now only dreaming about. It would also help us to stay in the present moment.

The ultimate goal was to have something called a "direct experience." I was not really sure what that meant but was told our truth would be revealed to us.

The technique we were to work with was called a *dyad,* which involved two people sitting across from each other. We were to look into each other's eyes, open our hearts, and listen, without any judgment at all, to whatever the other person wanted to talk about or confess. Our only response was to be "Thank you."

We took turns doing the dyad. When it was my turn, I was to focus only on me, look inside my heart, and be totally in the moment. I was to share whatever popped into my head, anything I needed to get off my chest, while someone listened to me non-judgmentally and lovingly said thank you. Little did I know this technique was going to be repeated over and over again many times throughout the weekend.

During the weekend, we also did several different types of meditations, or "contemplations," as they were called. Contemplations meant doing everything in complete silence, our only focus being on the sound of our own breath. We did walking contemplations, eating contemplations, and resting contemplations.

Yes, they did allow us to have naps. This and the walking were the best part for me. We took walks outside in the crisp morning air and at night, with the moon and stars shining and sparkling above us. At the end of the day, we had sleeping meditation, which meant we went to our rooms silently and then straight to bed. I was not allowed to talk to my roommates till Tuesday morning.

One evening, we were outside doing a walking contemplation. It was a cool, crisp night. Huge snowflakes were falling from the sky. Majestic mountains surrounded us, although in the dark I couldn't really see them. But I could feel their presence, as if they were watching over me.

I was walking in the newly fallen snow. All I could hear was crunch, crunch, crunch; everything else was so quiet and peaceful. I started to really focus on the sound my footsteps were making in the snow, and suddenly I realized it was the snow and me together, making this crunching sound. At that moment I realized how significant I was. I was creating this beautiful sound in the same way I was creating my life!

Breaking Through

I had a few more breakthroughs during these dyads and contemplations, which really helped me release many of my beliefs and resentments. In the dyads, I talked about how my first grade teacher had made me believe there was something wrong with me. I talked about the nine-year-old girl who had felt as if she didn't matter when she wasn't acknowledged in helping save Seanna from the dogs. I talked about the pain I had felt through my depression and not being able to have children and how inadequate I felt as a woman because of it. I talked about how guilty I felt for hurting Wes so badly.

It was like peeling an onion. I felt totally safe revealing to whatever person was sitting in front of me all the years of negative, twisted, poisonous thinking that had been going on in my head. I learned through this process *I am significant* and *there is nothing wrong with me*. I am unique and perfect exactly the way I am.

At one point, I even stood up on my chair and shouted, "I'm okay! There is nothing wrong with me! I do matter!" Everyone who heard me acknowledged me and said, "Yes, you do!" It was the most liberating and freeing feeling I have ever experienced. I have never felt insignificant or that I didn't matter since.

As Saturday and Sunday passed, the more I worked through the process, the fewer things came up for me. By Sunday night I was dreading every minute. I was bored, the days were long, and I felt like a captive. I was tired of this exercise, and I wanted to go home.

On Monday morning I woke up and thought, *Only one more day of this. I can't wait till this day is over. I can't wait to get out of here!"* I didn't want to quit, because I'm not a quitter. I thought, *If I can just get through this day, it will be okay.*

Then I remembered the man I'd partnered with Friday evening, Robin. I remembered him because he had been so positive. I was reminded that I teach this stuff and that, at that moment, I was being very negative. It was then that I made the intention to make the very best of this last day. I was going to have a direct experience!

I had seen several other people claim to have this direct experience throughout the weekend. I'd been a bit skeptical and wondered if they were faking it. But they looked so incredibly happy and full of joy. I didn't understand exactly what had gone on, but whatever they had, I wanted it. So with a different attitude, I gave it my all.

The first couple of dyads in the morning were very positive. I was regularly having visions during the process; for example, when asked by my partner to "Tell me who you are," I saw myself as a woman, a teenager, and a baby still in the womb waiting to be born. I also had a vision of myself being held in the palm of God's hands.

I didn't know what this meant, but as the process continued, I was able to get more and more relaxed, more and more into the moment, and more and more into my contemplation. I kept seeing a wall of glass, and on the other side of the glass was this magnificent light. I wasn't sure what the light was, but I knew I wanted to receive it. I wanted to break the glass.

At one point I visualized my nose sticking through the glass, which was now very pliable, almost like saran wrap. I closed my eyes for a few minutes and was totally in the moment, focusing on my body. Suddenly I felt a rush of energy, which started from my head and went all the way down to my toes. I had had a headache, and my shoulders had been very stiff and sore after hours of sitting in a chair. But after this rush of energy, all my aches were completely gone. I felt as if I had had the best workout of my life. My body felt limp; it felt like a full-body orgasm. It was amazing. It was WOW!

It was then time for our break. I asked Stephen, the facilitator, what this feeling was. "Is this what you mean by direct experience?" I asked. He explained that sometimes our bodies get these bursts of energy and that, "No, this was not a direct experience. You will know without question when you have it," he said.

After the break we continued with a new partner in another dyad. Again, I was able to easily get into the moment and focus only on my body. Then it happened: the most amazing experience of my life! I felt this huge burst of energy, even more powerful than before. I felt myself bursting through the glass wall and could feel the warmth of the brilliant light I had seen before. It felt like a waterfall was gushing into my chest right at my heart. My chest felt as if it were wide open.

I had no control of my body whatsoever. I couldn't feel my body. I could feel my head and shoulders moving back into the chair from the pressure, but my body was moving on its own—I was not moving it. I started panting, gasping for air with short quick breaths, as if I couldn't get enough air. I smelt a very strong smell, which is weird because, number one, I have a very poor sense of smell, and number two, no scented products were allowed in the room.

Suddenly, all I felt was goodness going into my heart. Tears started streaming down my face. Helpers were walking around the room monitoring people, answering questions and assisting people with their dyads. Donna, one of the monitors, rushed over to me and kept asking me, "Who are you?" I didn't have the words to explain it.

I'm not sure how long it lasted, but it was wonderful. All I felt was joy and love and peace flowing through my body. I felt free from all my burdens. I felt as if my being filled the entire room and beyond. I was conscious, actually much more aware than I had ever been. It was the most beautiful feeling I had ever had in my life. I didn't want it to end.

It was now lunchtime, and I could hardly walk to the dining room. My body was listless, I felt like a rag doll, and I was vibrating. One girl came up to me and gave me a hug and said, "Congratulations." I wasn't sure why she was congratulating me, but she said, "I can feel your energy. I can see the love in your eyes." I still didn't really understand what had happened to me.

Even though we had had little to eat over those few days, I wasn't hungry at all. I hadn't been satisfied with the small portions the first couple of days, but by the third day, I was hardly ever hungry at meal times. I picked at my food, then sat in silence and just looked out at the beautiful, amazing mountains. They appeared so much bigger than before. Everything seemed like it was bigger, brighter, and more intensified.

I needed to know what had happened to me, so I went and talked to the monitor, Donna, who had helped me through the experience. I asked, "What just happened to me?" She kept asking me, "Who are you?" and I didn't know what to say. I told her about the energy I felt flowing into my body. Then she asked, "What was the energy coming into you?" I said, "It was Pure Love, it was Pure Joy, it was Pure Truth." She just nodded her head in understanding. It was then that I realized what had happened, and I proceeded to bawl my eyes out. I told her I wasn't hungry and she said it was because I was full of spirit.

I finally knew who I was. I now knew that I am the source, I am love, I am truth, and it is running through my body all the time. I knew the truth—my truth and the truth of the Universe. I am one with God, I am one with the Universe, and my body is just a vessel.

My spirit lives forever. My spirit is everyone's spirit; my spirit is in the mountains and trees and stars. I am everything. I am all people. I now knew answers to the questions I had been searching for my entire life. We are all connected with all human beings and nature and everything in the universe by one loving energy. This energy I now knew to be God.

Because I hadn't been present to my own life, I had blocked all of this. Once I peeled away the layers of my "stuff," I was able to let it all pass through. I am so blessed. I am so grateful. I am complete. I have freedom. I am in control. I can do anything. I still have my "stuff," but I've been able to climb right through it. My "stuff" is what makes me who I am. All of my experiences make me unique. I am spirit having a human experience, and I chose this body to do it with.

This is what the yogis, saints, and sages all speak about. For many, it takes years of meditation to get to this state of bliss—and I found it in a weekend. Many others at the seminar also became enlightened, or "illuminated," as it was called. I have been awakened. I am blessed. I have lost my religion! No religion I have ever been taught compares to this; I have found true spirituality.

Enlightenment for Everyone

I once thought only Jesus or Mother Theresa or Buddha knew this powerful source, but the source is in everyone; we all can have enlightenment.

Elizabeth Gilbert, in her book *Eat, Pray, Love,* writes of her experience becoming one with the Divine. Some of the words she used to describe it are: "I am suddenly transported through the portal of the universe and taken to the center of God's palm . . . . It was the deepest love I'd ever experienced, beyond anything I could have previously imagined . . . . Why have I been chasing happiness my whole life when bliss was here the entire time?"

And as she "slid back down to earth" she heard God's unspoken message, "You may return here once you have fully come to understand that you are always here."

In his book *Power vs. Force*, David R. Hawkins, MD, writes about how when he was young he was caught in a blizzard and buried himself in a snow bank to stay warm. This is his experience:

> The shivering stopped and was replaced by delicious warmth . . . and then a state of peace beyond all description. This was accompanied by a suffusion of light and a Presence of infinite love, what had no beginning and no end . . . I became oblivious of the physical body and surroundings as my awareness fused with this all-present illuminated state. The mind grew silent; all thought stopped. An infinite Presence was all that was or could be, and it was beyond time and description. (p. 10)

Sharing the Love

A few months after Wes and I split up, I started dating again. I signed up for online dating and was chatting with a man whose spiritual qualities I was attracted to. We had long conversations about spirituality, and he confided that he had once had a very powerful spiritual experience. I said, "Really? I have too."

We decided to meet for supper. We were excited to share our stories. We sat down to eat and immediately started talking about spirituality. I described to him my experience at Nakodi Lodge. As I told him how it had felt like water gushing into my heart, he kept nodding his head. "Yes, that's exactly what I felt," he said.

Then I proceeded to tell him how my heart had opened up and all I could feel was pure . . . "Love!" he finished the sentence for me.

I was elated. Someone understands, some average Joe just like me gets it! It felt so good to share it with him. I hadn't told many people about my experience, as I was afraid people were going to think I had gone off the deep end and completely lost it—that they were going to lock me up. In fact, even writing this book is scary knowing some people may think differently of me.

But the day of my experience, one of the monitors, a well respected yogi master, told me, "Carla, you now have a job to do. You now have to share this love with everyone you come in contact with. Give it away, because there is more than enough for everyone, because it is constantly flowing in and through you."

I believe this is why I had this experience: to share it with others. So hopefully they too can know who they are and the love that resides within them.

CHAPTER 13

LIVING HEAVEN
HERE ON EARTH

You must learn a new way to think,
before you can master a new way to be.

~Marianne Williamson

For many years now, I have had the good fortune to study with mentors and teachers who've helped me find happiness and feel whole again. In this chapter I want to share with you some of the things I've learned. I hope this information helps you to begin your journey of awakening and self-discovery, as it did for me.

I want to stress that I am not a doctor or psychologist. I'm not saying that if you do what I have done, you will no longer need medication or therapy. What I share here is simply what worked for me, in conjunction with treatment from my physician and psychologists.

Everyone has times in their life when things don't go as they think they should, when tragedy strikes, or when sadness overcomes them. When this sadness extends for a period of time, it can become debilitating, robbing you of the happiness you deserve. But you can do things to overcome this sadness, to feel joy and find meaning in your life again, just as I have. Everyone is different. You just need to find what works for you, and do it.

The Answer is Energy

Over the last ten years of studying many success and spiritual gurus, I discovered that all of them are saying the same thing. They use different words to describe it, but the essential teaching is: what you focus on grows stronger. If you focus on the negative, that's what you'll get more of. If you focus on what's positive and good, you'll attract more good.

How does this work? The answer is energy. Let's look at how energy manifests itself in our lives.

The belief that there is a higher power, or energy, which flows to and through us and is the beginning of all creation and existence, has been the basis of religion and spirituality from the beginning of time. Even science agrees this energy exists. It can be referred to as Source, God, Creator, Universe, Spirit, or Higher Power, whatever makes most sense or is comfortable for you. For me, God is most comfortable and the term I prefer to use.

Science has proved that everything is made of energy, and this energy forms matter. Molecules moving at different speeds form different types of matter. A glass of water, for example, can be solid, liquid, or gas, depending on how fast the molecules are moving.

Electricity is a powerful source of energy we're all familiar with. Where does electricity come from? Do you know? We can plug in a 25-watt bulb and get a little bit of light, or we can plug in a 40-watt bulb, which gives us a little more light, but if we plug in a 100-watt bulb, this lights up the entire room. Do you think that if you plugged in a 500-watt bulb, the power source would still be there? Of course it would be.

You and I also have access to a very powerful source of universal energy that flows to and through us. We are to this universal source the same as a light bulb is to electricity, and, like electricity, we don't know where it comes from or how it works—it's just there. We can resist it and block it, or we can open ourselves up to it and let it flow through.

This energy is unlimited, in the same way our potential is unlimited, and it is only our own thoughts and limiting beliefs that prevent us from being anything we want to be. We have the power and potential to live a life that is amazing and unbelievable if we are open to it.

Our thoughts are also energy. The feelings or emotions we have regarding these thoughts cause movement or vibration. Have you ever walked into a room and immediately felt uncomfortable because of the people or surroundings? You would probably say you were getting "bad vibes" and decide to leave.

Or the opposite could be true. You could walk into a room that is beautifully decorated or filled with warm and friendly people laughing and having fun and feel "good vibes." It is this vibration that attracts things to us. Good thoughts and good energy vibrate at a certain frequency, and bad thoughts and energy vibrate at another. Good thoughts attract good things into our lives, and bad thoughts attract bad things. In other words, like attracts like. It's a universal law.

An example of this is my writing this book. I'd been thinking about it for a long time—for years, in fact. But I struggled with the thought of writing it, not knowing how to go about it. I kept putting it off. I didn't think I could do it. I also was afraid of revealing my deepest, darkest secrets to the world.

Then, a couple of months ago, I set the intention that in 2013 I was going to be a best selling author. Soon after I set that intention, my book flowed through me almost effortlessly. The tools and people I needed to support me miraculously showed up. For example, a course on How to Be a Best Selling Author, by Charmaine Hammond and Teresa de Grosbois, just happened to appear on my Facebook page one day. I then took the action step: I signed up for the course! Within weeks, my book went from a thought in my head to what you are now holding in your hands.

As humans we are made up of different forms of energy or vibrations. I would now like to focus on three that everyone is familiar with: body, intellect (mind), and spirit.

Spirit Comes First

The first one, and most important, is our spirit. This is the creative part of us. Our spirit is our subconscious, habits, beliefs, intuition, and self-image. This is essentially *who* we are.

Your spirit is the emotional and feeling part of you. When you feel good, you automatically feel happier. This indicates that you are in alignment with your destiny. When you feel bad, you are out of alignment, and it's time to readjust.

The best way I know to realign with spirit is meditating. Meditation is calming; it provides peace and tranquility—and it's the portal to enlightenment. There's no right or wrong way to meditate, and there are many different forms of meditation. As I mentioned in a previous chapter, you can do silent meditation, walking meditation, eating meditation, etc.

You may want to try different techniques till you find what works best for you. You may listen to audio recordings or music, say affirmations, chant, or just sit quietly. Most answers you're looking for come from the silence.

You may also attend church or read the Bible to reconnect with spirit.

Because your spirit is the feeling part of you, you need to do things that you find fun or bring you pleasure. When I was depressed, the things that once brought me joy no longer did. They were the last things I felt like doing; I had no interest in them at all. But I recognized this and forced myself to do the things I once enjoyed doing. And eventually I felt joy doing them again. It was hard work, but action will change your life. Doing the same things—or doing nothing—and expecting different results will keep you in the clouds of despair.

Our beliefs also prevent us from doing things that may bring us joy. Our beliefs are buried in our subconscious, based on things others have said or what we have said to ourselves. When we change these beliefs, we can do things we couldn't even imagine we could.

When I started running to lose weight, a friend of mine suggested that I sign up for a half-marathon. I said, "Are you crazy, lady? There is no way I could do a half-marathon."

Not long after, she convinced a fellow we worked with to do a half-marathon. This is a guy who never exercises, smokes a pack of cigarettes a day, and loves his beer! Without any training, he completed it. He did it only to prove to her that he could, but I knew if he could do it, I could do it too. So right after that, I signed up for my first half-marathon.

I went about it a little differently though—I trained for mine. It's hard to explain the feeling I had coming across that finish line. It was euphoria! I was so proud of myself! I had accomplished something I never thought in a million years I could do. As soon as I changed that belief, which was buried in my subconscious, running a half-marathon became a reality for me—not just once, but three times.

This is true for anything. I am now pushing my limits further and training for my first full marathon. I will do it even if I have to crawl over that finish line.

So do the unimaginable. Do whatever makes your heart sing and brings you joy. Do what you have always been wanting or saying you would like to do, because you can! Find your passions and follow them. Your passions are given to you for a reason. They are God's gift to you, and your gift to God is to share them with others.

Intellect (Mind): Choosing Thoughts That Feed Us

A

Thought

That

I

Think

Ultimately

Determines

Everything

~Phyllis Bennett

The next level of vibration is our mind, thoughts, ideas, imagination, memory, perception, and reasoning. The bottom line is: we can choose our thoughts and are 100% responsible for the thoughts we choose. As Shakespeare said, "Nothing is either good or bad, but thinking makes it so."

The thing that really helped me change my life was retraining my brain and making positive thinking a habit to replace the negative thinking I had been doing most of my life. To do this, the first thing I did, and something I highly recommend, was start a Gratitude Journal. Every evening before I went to bed, I would write five things that I was grateful for that day. In the beginning it was very hard for me to come up with five things. Now, it is much easier, and I can usually fill a page with ten or more reasons to be grateful. It really helps you focus on what is good in your life, rather than what is not.

Next, I started to pay close attention to my thoughts, and every time a negative thought came into my head, I'd say "erase" and replace it with an opposite, good, or positive thought.

It was difficult at first, as my old habits would take over. But the longer I practiced it, the easier it became—it's almost automatic for me now. Do I still have negative thoughts? Of course, all the time. I wouldn't be human if I didn't. But they happen much less often than before. And now I know when I'm feeling down or things aren't going the way I want them to, it's because of my thoughts. I then do whatever I can to get back into a positive thought pattern again.

You may be saying to yourself, well, that's all fine and good, but sometimes stuff happens and life unexpectedly throws you a curve ball, something totally out of your control that sends you spiraling down and is hard to find anything good about. It may seem so, but there is a positive side to everything. There has to be: it's another universal law. The law of polarity states that everything has an opposite. If there is up, there must be down; if there is left, there has to be right; if there is cold, then there needs to be hot.

Here's an example of being able to choose one perspective over another. My nine-year-old nephew Jesse was playing hockey in a tournament. He was the goalie that weekend—they won some games and lost some as well. After the weekend, his mom, Trish, asked him what game had been the most fun. He said, "The one we lost 14-1." She said "Really?" not expecting this answer at all. He said, "Yes, Mom, I made fifty-six saves in that game." Now that is what I call a positive attitude.

All events are neutral; it is our perception of them that gives them meaning.

We can't control everything that happens around us; the only thing we can control is how we react. We can allow an event to continue to make us suffer, or we can accept it, learn from it, and move on. Ask yourself, "If I hang on to this, am I willing to continue to suffer?" If the answer is yes, then continue doing what you're doing. If the answer is no, then deal with it, and ask yourself how you can turn it around to eliminate the suffering; the suffering will then fall away. You can remain bitter or you can get better, you choose.

When I was training to become a Passion Test Facilitator, a woman in the group shared with us how she had once been homeless. She was able to turn her life around and now operates an organization helping the homeless get back on their feet. She is loving her life and living her passion. If she had not gone through her experience, she would not have found her passion. In many cases, our true passions are revealed to us through our trials.

The same can be said for Chris. He needed to go to jail so he could turn his life around. In many cases, we need to hit bottom before we can find the courage to change.

Once I realized that all the crap I had gone through was a gift given to me so I could help others, my entire perspective changed. I needed to search my whole life for answers in order to find spirituality and awakening. I needed to have the experience of not being able to have children so I can now help others going through the same thing. I needed to go through hell to find happiness. When we help to make the lives of others richer, our lives become more meaningful.

Even in death there are positives. It may be hard to find them at first, but they're there. A couple of months after the retreat to Nakodi Lodge, my sister Phyllis and I were in Red Deer, Alberta running a half-marathon. After the race we received a devastating call. My niece Ashley had found her baby boy, Kayden, dead in his crib from Sudden Infant Death Syndrome (SIDS). He was six months old.

How could this happen? It was so hard for us to understand. Again another blow our family had to endure.

But this time I didn't blame God, as I had so many times before. I don't believe it was God who took him, but Kayden's own spirit that chose to leave this earth—for whatever reason, we'll never know. He chose Ashley to be his mom and our family to love him for the short time he was here, and he was here to teach us something. I also knew he was in a very beautiful place, as he was with others we had lost, like Dad and BJ, and I knew he was okay. This brought my family and me much comfort.

Following Kayden's death, my sister Kim and her daughter Ashley started a campaign to raise funds for SIDS. Their goal was to raise $5000; I could sense the passion my sister Kim had planning the event.

Over the course of several weeks people from the community came together, fully supporting their mission and bending over backwards to help them. The event grew larger than they ever expected. The local hockey team stepped in and brought in celebrities, the Hansen Brothers from the movie *Slapshot*, and donated a portion of the ticket sales to SIDS.

In the end they raised over $17,000 for the SIDS foundation, to raise awareness and help other parents who had lost children to SIDS. I told Kim, "This all happened because of the passion and love you put into this." It truly was a "God moment."

Instead of focusing on the tragedy of losing their children and the short time they had with them, both Koreen and Ashley celebrated the lives of their children. With the fundraiser for SIDS and Koreen's volunteer work with Victim Services, they honored their sons' lives and made them more meaningful. And by helping others, they helped heal themselves.

They will always grieve the loss of their children; the pain will never completely go away. But by finding joy and happiness again and living life to the fullest, they model what it means to make choices in favor of living.

Nourishing the Physical: Body and Environment

The last form of energy I want to cover is our body or physical form. Our bodies don't make us who we are—they're what we live in. Yet when it comes to healing, most people focus on our physical bodies and the physical world because they're tangible, the parts we can see and most easily understand.

Nurturing our body is something we hear about every day. Eat healthy, exercise, get lots of rest, blah, blah, blah. Well, folks, I'm going to tell you the same thing here. I now make nurturing my body with good healthy foods not only a priority in my life, but a necessity. I have noticed the food I eat affects my moods and the way I feel about myself. When I put unhealthy food into my body, my mood goes down and I have less energy.

The most important thing I did to lose one hundred pounds was to stop eating all foods that contained flour and sugar. I read labels on everything now. If something contains these two products, I avoid eating them as much as possible except for an occasional treat. I find when I eat foods like pasta, pizza, bread, baked goods, candy, etc., my body craves them and I can't get enough of them.

I truly believe obesity is due to food addiction—an addiction to flour and sugar. In my opinion they are poison to our bodies. A mantra I repeat to myself everyday is "sugar makes me crazy and flour makes me lazy." Cut them out and your health and your mood will improve exponentially.

My diet now consists mainly of vegetables, lean protein, fruit, dairy, and whole grains. I seldom crave unhealthy food and making healthy choices is now a habit for me. I have an abundance of energy as well.

Another thing I notice is how drinking alcohol affects me. Alcohol is a depressant. I have recognized that when I drink, my mood is lower for a day or two afterward. If you find yourself experiencing the same mood swings, you may want to consider drinking less alcohol.

Exercise is more medicine for our mood. Exercising at least thirty minutes three times a week, even if it's just a walk in the sunshine and fresh air, will elevate your mood, provide fuel for your body, and give you more energy. Our bodies and muscles need to move. When I exercise, I feel better about myself, sleep better, and am less stressed. Stress and an inadequate amount of sleep are known causes of depression.

It's not only our bodies that need nurturing—our physical environments need attention as well. Make your home your sanctuary. Surround yourself with beautiful and meaningful things, things that speak to your heart. Keep your home organized and uncluttered. Get rid of the chaos happening around you. Take everything you haven't used in the last year and give it to charity.

Decluttering is very freeing. It gives you greater clarity and a sense of order. Try cleaning out your clothes closet and getting rid of everything you haven't worn in a while or that doesn't fit anymore. Then observe how you feel afterwards. I guarantee you will feel better.

Bob Proctor says that he can tell how disorganized and stressful people's lives are just by looking in their vehicles. If your vehicle is dirty and full of garbage, chances are your life is in a bit of disarray. Clean it up and see how things change for you.

The show "Hoarders" is a perfect example of this. It demonstrates how people become overwhelmed and their lives become unmanageable. Once they clean up and organize their immediate surroundings, their entire life changes. Bob Proctor also says that you need to rid yourself of old and unwanted stuff to make room for new stuff. It's called the Vacuum Law of Prosperity.

Remember, everything is energy. Disorder and disarray harbor bad energy. Organization and cleanliness harbor good uplifting energy.

*   *   *

Our spirit, intellect (mind), and physical body are all forms of energy, or, put another way, three levels of awareness. To live a totally balanced life, we must give equal attention to all three levels. Things really started changing for me when I took my focus off my physical body and physical world and started focusing more on my spirit and the essence of who I was. When I focused on my spirit, I realized I could create anything I chose to, and my life began to take on a whole new meaning.

To put this into perspective, we need to ask the question, "What is the opposite of creating?" If we are not creating, we are disintegrating or dying. It is true for anything in nature. If you are not growing and creating, you are dying.

When I was depressed I, focused on my physical world and how awful it was. I didn't pay any attention to the bad thoughts I was thinking, and I certainly didn't pay attention to the spiritual part of me. Here's what I was doing:

P— Focusing on my physical body and physical world. I thought this was the only thing I had control over.

I— Paying very little attention to my thoughts (intellect). After years of thinking negatively, it was a habit for me, which was attracting all the negative things into my life.

S— Not acknowledging the spiritual side of me. I paid no attention to my spirit and just let my life happen, without having any realization I could control all of this.

Essentially I was PIS-ing my life away. I was eliminating all the goodness from my life, releasing it . . . down the drain.

After all my studying, I realized I had it all backwards—I needed to reverse things. So I started to focus more on my spirit and nurturing it. I also needed to pay more attention to my thoughts and feelings, and when I did, I found my life turned around very quickly. Here's what I did:

S— I started to nurture and focus on my spirit first and foremost. It is essentially who we are and is the most important of all.

I— I started paying attention to my intellect (mind). I started choosing thoughts and ensuring that the thoughts I focused on were positive. I made a conscious effort to erase all bad thoughts from my mind.

P— Last, but not least, I nurtured my physical body by providing it with good healthy food and exercise.

Look after your body, mind, and spirit. Nourish your body with healthy food, nurture your spirit, and challenge your mind.

Having a balance between these three states of being will give you energy, vitality, and happiness.

All three are connected. All three need nurturing for us to live happy, healthy lives. Once I started SIP'ing and filling myself with goodness, I began to feel fulfilled. I found that heaven was just a SIP away. My cup was overflowing.

CONCLUSION

When I stand before thee at the day's end
thou shalt see my scars and know
that I had my wounds and also my healing.

~Rabindranath Tagore

If you are looking for an instant cure for depression or obesity, you will never find it. If you are looking for something easy, this isn't it. It is hard work. It takes determination and persistence. But anything in life worth having is hard work—and it is absolutely worth it. Here are some of my final thoughts.

Stop blindly following the masses and living a mediocre life. Stop worrying what others think of you. Start living authentically; take control and create the life you dream about and deserve. It is your birthright to live a magnificent life. It is there for the taking for you and for everyone.

Start consciously living your life, being aware and awake. Wake up and smell the roses, as they say. Life is not fair—get over it, stop whining, and start living. Do what you need to do to get what you want. Staying at the pity party will only keep you down. Pick yourself up and start again. Change your victim mentality to one of responsibility, accountability, and empowerment.

My life did a complete one-hundred-eighty-degree turn when I made the decision that I wanted more and would no longer accept being less than my very best. I then started taking the necessary steps that changed my life forever. Make the decision to do it and take action. This is probably one of the most important tips I can give you. Be willing to do whatever it takes to make the changes you desire.

Not making a decision is still a decision. So decide what you need to do—then take action steps one by one, even if you don't know at first what they all are.

A great example of this is making a decision to go on a vacation. You begin to put money aside so that you can go. You call a travel agent to book your hotel and flight. You make arrangements to get time off work. You drive to the airport to catch your flight.

You made a decision, you took action, and you arrived at your destination. This is true for all situations in life. Make the decision, decide what you want, and take the action steps towards it. You may not know what the steps are, but they will be revealed to you as you go. Have faith the universe can and will give you more than you could ever dream possible, and it will!

For so many years I tried so hard to feel accepted and fit in, but what I really wanted was to step out and stand out. The only way to do that was to be true to who I really was.

I have learned many lessons on my journey, far too many to include in one book. Some have been simple, but the major ones have been shared with you here. I learned from my first grade teacher, Mrs. Elliot, not to allow the words of another to define who you are. Not to allow anyone to take away your power. That you are perfect in God's eyes and are here for a reason, to be spectacular just by being you.

My experience saving Seanna from the dog taught me that I needed to let go of my resentments and not allow them to diminish my life and who I am. I had to forgive in order to let go. It was no one's intention to cause me pain, but my perspective that was making me believe it. By changing my perception, I was able to release the pain and move on.

When I decided to go back to school, I remember thinking, *I will never allow myself to be dependent on someone else to support me. I will find a job where I will make enough money to support myself.* Not knowing it at the time, I was really setting an intention. My career has provided me a good source of income, and I have always been able to support myself because I made that intention and decision so many years ago.

Why was I not able to have children? I don't know the answer to that, but I believe it's because I was meant to help other couples struggling with infertility, which is why I have committed half of all proceeds of this book to an organization called Generations of Hope, which provides financial assistance to couples for in vitro fertilization. Also, I think it helped me to focus on Chris and be a better mother to him.

The deaths of BJ, Dad, and Kayden not only saved my life but brought me closer to God and my family, and helped me realize that our connection to the spiritual world is forever and that our loved ones are always here with us.

My weight loss was not about the weight at all. I had to learn to love myself again before I was able to accept who I was, no matter what my body size. The hunger I had was not for food, but for a spiritual connection to God, mankind, Mother Earth, and all living things.

The end of my marriage wasn't a failure; it was two people who loved each other very deeply but who ended up on different paths, wanting different things. We had a mutual understanding that we could love enough to let each other go. We are not meant to be in relationships where we are no longer happy, and the knot I felt in my gut for so long was my intuition, or God's way of telling me it was okay to leave. I believe that no one should stay with another out of obligation, because when both are set free, both can find even more love.

And this brings me to my final point.

It is love that helped me and my family through many hardships. It kept us close, being there for one another and supporting each other through tough times. It helped us cope with the loss of our father and sons and gave us the strength to go on.

Love is what helped Chris overcome his addiction and now live a happy, healthy life. Wes and I loved and supported him every step of the way. We would not and did not give up on him!

Love is what brought me happiness again; learning to love myself. I now know that I am as beautiful and perfect as a butterfly, a flower, a snowflake, a sunset, a mountain, an ocean, a newborn baby, and all of God's creations—just as I AM!

LOVE! It is there when we come into this world, and it is there when we go out. It is the most powerful of all emotions. It is all that matters!

I am love, you are love, and God is love—pure love!

Epilogue

Begin today!
Declare out loud to the universe
that you are willing to let go of struggle
and eager to learn through joy!

~Sarah Ban Breathnach

I t is May, 2013, spring time; the time of new growth and new beginnings. Outside, the snow has melted and my rose bush has new leaves—and soon will have roses.

I am so amazed and grateful for my wonderful life. I now live a life of purpose with meaning and fulfillment. My heart is full of joy and I have peace. I rarely feel down or depressed. And if I do, I know that I am not aligned with my true self and know what to do to get back on track again.

When things happen out of my control, I look for the good or the lesson that's there to teach me and know that this too shall pass.

I am no longer fighting my destiny but going with the flow and allowing God's guidance to show me.

I have been able to maintain a healthy weight for six years and have good eating and exercise habits.

I continue to attend seminars and plan to do two or three a year for the rest of my life to continue on my journey. No matter where I am in life, I know there is always more to learn.

Wes and I are now divorced but remain good friends. He is doing well and in a happy relationship.

Chris has been drug free for over five years. He does well at his job and is a journeyman in his trade. He is a wonderful father to a beautiful baby boy, my grandson, Braeden, and will be marrying the love of his life, Amanda, in July of 2013.

I still feel the pain of not having children, but I have accepted it. There are times I still shed tears and yearn for the baby I never had. It is in those moments I give all my love to Chris, Braeden, my beautiful nieces and nephews, and their babies.

I have moved back to my childhood home and am reacquainting with lifelong friends. I feel so at home and at peace here. I have met an amazing man Mark, that I love with *ALL* of my heart. My life is amazing. I am happy!

When I didn't know what else to do, I let go—and remarkable things happened when I surrendered. Each day is a gift, and each moment precious. Every day when we awake we have a choice to begin again and celebrate this wonderful life that God has given us. I had to go through the depths of hell to find heaven here on earth, but I wake up every day and realize, as the saying goes, that today is the first day of the rest of my life!

And I'm going to make the most of it.

Just remember in the winter far beneath the bitter snow
Lies a seed that with the suns love, in the spring becomes the rose.

The Beginning . . .

RESOURCES

Set a goal to achieve something that is so big,
so exhilarating, that it excites you and scares you
at the same time.

~Bob Proctor

T his section contains a summary of all the things I did to find happiness, most of which I continue to do every day. They are my priority; the times when I haven't made them a priority, I slowly slipped back into old negative habits. Then when I started doing them again, my life improved almost instantly.

Included here are:

- 10 Ways to Find Happiness
- Ideal Life Exercise
- Daily Gratitude Exercise
- Yearly Exercise
- Recommended Reading
- Programs and Seminars

10 Ways to Find Happiness

1. Meditate

The number one thing I recommend to nurture your spirit is to meditate. Meditation is calming. It provides peace and tranquility, and is the portal to enlightenment. You may want to try different techniques till you find what works best for you—there is no right or wrong way to do it. You may listen to audio recordings or music, say affirmations, chant, or just sit quietly for your meditation practice. Most answers you are looking for come from the silence.

2. Connect with Nature

I also spend time outdoors, going for walks and getting in touch with nature. I listen to the birds, breathe in the fresh air, stop and smell the roses, and appreciate all the beauty Mother Earth has to offer.

3. Do Things you Enjoy

I have bubble baths by candlelight. I read lots of positive inspirational books; there are literally thousands out there. I have listed in the Appendix some very good books that have helped me. Watch an inspiring movie (non-violent!). *The Secret, Pay it Forward, The Bucket List,* and *The Shift* with Wayne Dyer are some very good ones. I also listen to beautiful, soothing music that moves my soul. I sing at the top of my lungs, I dance like no one is watching (and when no one is watching!).

Other things you can do are go to church, read the Bible, sit in a park and watch children play, listen to their laughter, go to a spiritual retreat, play games with your family, go fishing, quading, horse back riding, laugh—anything to have fun!

4. Start a Gratitude Journal

One of the biggest things I did to change my thoughts from negative to positive was keeping a gratitude journal. I started focusing on what was good in my life rather than what was bad. What you focus on grows stronger, as that is where the energy goes.

Each night before I go to bed, I write down things that have happened throughout my day that I am grateful for. This was very difficult in the beginning; I often thought I had nothing to be grateful for. I had trouble coming up with five. But as time went on, it became easier, and those five things turned to six, seven, and now I write down ten things I am grateful for every day.

It can be anything from I'm thankful for: the sunshine, green grass my warm bed, and food on my table. A really good book to help you do this is *The Magic*, by Rhonda Byrne. It takes you through thirty days of gratitude. You'll notice big changes even after thirty days. Try it! This will be one of the most important things you can do to start living a more positive and fulfilling life.

5. Affirmations

I recorded myself saying affirmations and I listened to them every day. Examples of affirmations I love follow on page 98.

6. Surround Yourself with Positive People

As I mentioned in previous chapters, I attend a lot of personal development seminars and workshops. I continue to do this to rejuvenate myself on a regular basis. Not only do I learn something, but I also get to hang out with positive, like-minded people and meet new friends along the way.

There are many seminars being offered today that are changing people's lives and giving people hope and freedom to be the people they were meant to be. Participate in as many seminars as possible. I have listed some very good ones in the appendix as well, all of which I have participated in. I have met some very successful, influential, loving, caring people in these seminars and have made good friends through them. Immerse yourself in this valuable information. You owe it to yourself to invest in these.

7. Create a Vision Board

Another helpful tool is a Vision Board. Seeing pictures of your heart's desires helps you to hold the vision in your mind. When the vision is in your mind, it manifests in your life. Thoughts become things!

This can be done a number of ways. Take photos of the things you want in your life from magazines, newspapers, or the Internet, and paste them onto a bulletin board or poster board. Put the board somewhere where you'll be able to see it every day. Mine is on the wall in front of my desk so that I can look at it daily. You can also make a movie that contains visions of your heart's desires; make sure to watch it on a regular basis so your visions will be locked in your mind's eye and always present. If you hold your vision, it will soon manifest into your desires.

8. Write Down your Goals and Ideal Life

Write out what your ideal life looks like. For every facet of your life, relationships, career, financial, health, environment, etc. write out what it will look like if money and time were of no significance, and then keep those visions in your head and focus your energy towards them.

Another trick I use is to write out cheques to myself for things I want. I use an old chequebook and write out the amount of money it will take to purchase what I desire. Once I receive what I desire, I write on the back, "Thank you for the money." I am amazed at how quickly I am able to accumulate the things I want to acquire. So far this year I have received a new house and kitchen, and I've paid off my vehicle.

9. Eat a Healthy Diet

Eat plenty of vegetables and fruit. Choose lean proteins such as chicken, beef, eggs, and fish. Eliminate all processed foods. If it's white or comes in a box, don't eat it. Check labels. Many foods you think are healthy are full of sugar.

10. Exercise

Move your body. Not only does it help with stress, it fills it with nourishing oxygen and creates more flexibility. Start small by going for short walks. Set goals each week to go a little farther. Do what you enjoy doing—walking, cycling, yoga, dancing—anything to get your body moving. Exercise also provides feel-good endorphins to your brain.

Affirmations

1. I am a total success.
2. Things always go my way in life.
3. All of my efforts bring rich rewards.
4. I set high goals for myself that I'm able to attain.
5. I am a warm and friendly person and people are naturally drawn to me.
6. People seek me out to do business with me.
7. I am totally relaxed and confident in making presentations.
8. I feel positive at all times and people respond to me in a positive way.
9. I powerfully attract more and more customers to my business.
10. My positive and enthusiastic attitude is infectious.
11. People want to buy from me.
12. My customers recommend me to others.
13. The number of my customers is increasing daily.
14. My sales are increasing dramatically.
15. My income level is rising higher and higher.
16. I am a success at everything I do.
17. Everything goes my way and works out positively for me.
18. I have a magnetic personality and attract people socially and in business.
19. More and more money is coming to me.
20. All of my efforts are productive.
21. I believe in myself completely.
22. I am attaining my goals—nothing can deter me from my goals.
23. My income level is increasing dramatically.
24. I have total confidence and know I am a winner in life.
25. Money comes to me easily and frequently.

26. I deserve riches and success—prosperity is mine.
27. I speak and communicate well with others.
28. I always say the right things to my clients.
29. The suggestions I give my clients always help them.
30. I make sound decisions quickly.
31. I am a good listener.
32. I have a perfect memory.
33. I have many friends.
34. I am perfectly healthy.
35. I have a slim body and am physically fit.
36. I love my partner deeply and receive love in return.
37. I have wonderful relationships with my son and all of my family.
38. I have peace, serenity, and joy, and I live in harmony with spirit at all times.
39. My life is full; I love my life.
40. I am witty and have a great sense of humor.
41. I laugh many times a day.
42. I am whole, perfect, strong, powerful, loving, and happy.
43. I have good judgment and my decisions are always right for me.
44. Ideas come into my head exactly when I need them.
45. I always choose the right words.
46. I am very intelligent and wise, and my intellectual faculties are highly developed.
47. I am beautiful.
48. I have fun at everything I do.
49. I thrive in my business.
50. I thrive in life.

Ideal Life Exercise

This exercise is similar to a vision board and will help you get clear on what you want your ideal life to be like.

If you could be, do, and have anything you wanted; if money and time were no object; and if everyone in your life supported you, what would your life be like? Picture that: What are your heart's desires? Where are you living, what are you doing, what are your passions, and who are you with? What will you have accomplished? What will they say about you at your 100th birthday party? Write down what your ideal life would look like. Dream big—there are absolutely no limits!.

Consider all areas of your life: spiritual, financial, career, relationships, health, environment, etc.

Example of my Ideal Life

Spiritual—I start with this one because it's the most important. I meditate/sit quietly for at least fifteen minutes every day, I go to church every Sunday, I read one chapter from the Bible every week, I pray every night before I go to bed, I live in the present moment 90% of the time, I live in joy and peace 95% of the time, I go on a spiritual retreat once a year, etc. Whatever you want your life to look like spiritually, write it down.

Financial—I am making $1,000,000 a year, I have several streams of income, I have $10 million dollars in investments., I own everything outright, I have financial freedom.

Career—I love what I do and am following my passion, I have several successful businesses, my Internet marketing business is very successful, I have a best-selling book, I speak to thousands of people all over the world.

Relationships—I am living with my true love and soul mate; I have a very loving, supportive, and happy relationship with my partner; I spend two hours of quality time with my partner a day; I spend two hours of quality time with my children every day; I spend one day a week with my grandchildren; I spend two hours a week with a good friend, etc.

Environment—I am living in a beautiful cottage on the beach in a tropical destination. I am able to travel wherever and whenever I choose.

Entertainment—I spend much of my time golfing, I have written several books that are on the *New York Times* best-seller list, I volunteer my time with numerous charities, I am an international speaker sharing my message and raising awareness about depression and infertility.

Daily Gratitude Exercise

Thank you for this day. (Add date.)

What I am grateful for:

_____

_____

_____

_____

_____

What brought me joy today:

_____

_____

_____

_____

_____

Affirmations:

_____

_____

_____

_____

_____

What I did for my spirit today:

_____

_____

_____

_____

_____

What I did to have a healthy body today:

_____

_____

_____

_____

_____

What I did to reach my goals:

_____

_____

_____

_____

_____

My successes for today are:

_____

_____

_____

_____

_____

Quote of the day:

_____

_____

_____

_____

_____

Yearly Exercise

For example:

December 31, 2012

Write down all the goals you intend to accomplish for 2013:

_____

_____

_____

_____

_____

_____

December 31, 2013

Look at the goals you set at the beginning of 2013. Write down all the goals you accomplished and any other successes you have had this year.

_____

_____

_____

_____

_____

_____

Celebrate! Do something nice for yourself, buy something for yourself, do something that brings you joy.

Recommended Reading

Think and Grow Rich—Napoleon Hill

You Were Born Rich—Bob Proctor

Anything by Wayne Dyer

The Passion Test—Janet Bray Attwood and Chris Attwood

The Secret—Rhonda Byrne

The Power—Rhonda Byrne

The Magic—Rhonda Byrne

Power vs. Force—David Hawkins

Eat Pray Love—Elizabeth Gilbert

Conversations with God (Volumes 1, 2 and 3)—Neale Donald Walsh

Programs and Seminars

The Creator's Code—Jay Fisset, Ray-ann Wood-Schatz
www.creatorscode.com

The Creator's Code is a global movement of conscious creators, people who are committed to evolving themselves, their communities, and, ultimately, the world. We hold the space that every person has their own answers and is already whole, complete, and infinitely capable. We hold the space that some people are a perfect fit for the values, energy, mission, and intention of The Creator's Code and some are not . . . yet; we hold the space that they too will find their way . . .

LifeSuccess—Bob Proctor
www.bobproctor.com

One of the most sought-after speakers in the world for professional coaching and company seminars, and a teacher in the wildly popular film *The Secret*, Proctor is considered one of the living masters and teachers of the Law of Attraction. For more than forty years, Bob Proctor has focused his work and teachings on helping people use the power of their mind to achieve prosperity, rewarding relationships, and spiritual awareness. He is the best-selling author of *You Were Born Rich* and has transformed the lives of millions through his books, seminars, courses, and personal coaching.

Peak Potentials—Adam Markel, President
www.peakpotentials.com

Peak Potentials is one of the fastest growing business and personal success training companies in North America. We specialize in "inner world principles for real world success." Our goal is to help people identify and overcome the hidden obstacles that hold them back from reaching their full potential in terms of both success and happiness. So far we have helped over 1,000,000 people around the world transform their lives.

By utilizing high-impact, breakthrough processes, our participants experience both immediate and long-term changes that include higher incomes, greater net worth, better relationships, true power, and a sense of inner peace.

Peak Potentials' seminars are taught using high-involvement, accelerated learning techniques that allow participants to learn faster, remember more, and have tons of fun (all while dramatically enhancing their lives).

If there is one word to describe the Peak Potentials philosophy, that word is "ACTION!" Our seminars are extraordinary; however, we believe it's what you do and what happens in your life after the seminar that really counts!

Warrior Sage—Satyan Raja
www.warriorsage.com

The Path of the Warrior Sage is for you if you are committed and willing to do anything and everything to transcend a life half lived, and to give your full potential to the world, so that you awaken every morning, burning with the excitement to create your highest vision of life that day, and so that when you die, you die complete, having given your deepest gifts daily.

Food Addicts Anonymous
www.foodaddicts.org

We are an international fellowship of men and women who have experienced difficulties in life as a result of the way we used to eat. We joined FA because we were obsessed with food. We find that we need this program of recovery and the fellowship of others who share our problem in order to stop abusing food and to begin living fulfilling lives. Through shared experience and mutual support, we help each other to recover from the disease of food addiction.

Our program of recovery is based on the Twelve Steps and Twelve Traditions of Alcoholics Anonymous. We make use of AA principles to gain freedom from addictive eating. There are no dues, fees, or weigh-ins at FA meetings. Membership is open to anyone who wants help with food.

The Work—Byron Katie
www.thework.com

The Work of Byron Katie is a way of identifying and questioning the thoughts that cause all the anger, fear, depression, addiction, and violence in the world. Experience the happiness of undoing those thoughts through The Work, and allow your mind to return to its true, awakened, peaceful, creative nature.

Kieron Sweeney's Global Web Show
www.KieronTV.com

Provides daily twenty-minute coaching sessions designed to enrich your mind with his personally designed coaching, which has helped thousands of people double and triple their income and create better relationships and health.

BIBLIOGRAPHY

Hawkins, David R., MD, PhD. *Power vs. Force: The Hidden Determinants of Human Behavior.* Sedona, Arizona: Veritas Publishing,1995

Gilbert, Elizabeth. *Eat Pray Love.* New York: Penguin Group Inc., 2006

ABOUT THE AUTHOR

Carla Coates has been studying personal development for more than ten years and has transformed her life completely.

She has trained with Bob Proctor, Chris and Janet Bray Attwood, Stephen Garrett, Ray-Ann Wood-Schatz, Jay Fisset, Kieron Sweeney and many other transformational leaders.

She is a Certified LifeSuccess Consultant, Passion Test Facilitator, speaker, and author. She has lead mastermind groups and facilitated her own workshops and seminars in the personal development field. She is President and CEO of her own business Goal Mind Ventures, that includes business and real-estate investing.

She also has a longstanding career in the health care field. Her passion is to inspire others to transform their lives as she has. She lives in Alberta, Canada.

CPSIA information can be obtained at www.ICGtesting.com
Printed in the USA
LVOW080652250613

340013LV00002BA/21/P